Socially Engaged Buddhism

DIMENSIONS OF ASIAN SPIRITUALITY

Shinto: The Way Home
Thomas P. Kasulis

Chan Buddhism
Peter D. Hershock

Korean Spirituality
Don Baker

Ancient Chinese Divination
Stephen L. Field

Socially Engaged Buddhism
Sallie B. King

Socially Engaged Buddhism

SALLIE B. KING

Dimensions of Asian Spirituality

UNIVERSITY OF HAWAI'I PRESS

Honolulu

Editor's Preface

ABOUT THIS SERIES

The University of Hawai'i Press has long been noted for its scholarly publications in, and commitment to, the field of Asian Studies. The present volume is the fifth in a series initiated by the Press in keeping with that commitment, Dimensions of Asian Spirituality.

It is a most appropriate time for such a series. A number of the world's religions—major and minor—originated in Asia, continue to influence significantly the lives of almost half of the world's peoples, and should now be seen as global in scope, reach, and impact, with rich and varied resources for every citizen of the twenty-first century to explore.

Religion is at the heart of every culture. To be sure, cultures have also been influenced by climate, geology, and the consequent patterns of economic activity they have developed for the production and distribution of goods. Only a very minimal knowledge of physical geography is necessary to understand why African sculptors largely employed wood as their medium while their Italian Renaissance brethren usually worked with marble. But while necessary for understanding cultures—not least our own—matters of geography and economics will not be sufficient. Wood and marble are also found in China, yet Chinese sculptors carved Confucian sages, Daoist immortals, and bodhisattvas from their materials, not *chiwaras* or *pietas*.

In the same way, a mosque, synagogue, cathedral, stupa, and pagoda may be equally beautiful, but they are beautiful in different ways, and the differences cannot be accounted for merely on the basis of the materials used in their construction; their beauty, their ability to inspire awe and to invite contemplation, rests largely on the religious view of the world—and the place of human beings in that world—that inspired and is expressed in their architecture.

Thus the spiritual dimensions of a culture are reflected significantly

distorted. When studying other religions, most people are strongly inclined to focus on cosmological and ontological questions, asking, What do these people believe about how the world came to be, how it is, and where it is heading? Do they believe in ghosts? Immortal souls? A creator god?

Answering these and related metaphysical questions is of course necessary for understanding and appreciating fully the specific forms and content of the art, music, architecture, rituals, and traditions inspired by the specific religion under study. But the sensitive—and sensible—student will bracket the further question of whether the metaphysical pronouncements are literally true; we must attend carefully to the metaphysics (and theologies) of the religions we study, but questions of their literal truth should be set aside to concentrate on a different question: How could a thoughtful, thoroughly decent human being subscribe to and follow these beliefs and attendant practices?

Studied in this light, we may come to see and appreciate how each religious tradition provides a coherent account of a world not fully amenable to human manipulation, nor perhaps even to full human understanding. The metaphysical pronouncements of the world's religions of course differ measurably from faith to faith, and each has had a significant influence on the physical expressions of the respective faith in synagogues, stupas, mosques, pagodas, and cathedrals. Despite these differences among the buildings, however, the careful and sensitive observer can see the spiritual dimensions of human life that these sacred structures share and express, and in the same way we can come to see and appreciate the common spiritual dimensions of each religion's differing metaphysics and theology. While the several religious traditions give different answers to the question of the meaning *of* life, they all provide a multiplicity of similar guidelines and spiritual disciplines to enable everyone to find meaning *in* life, in this world.

By plumbing the spiritual depths of other religious traditions, then, we may come to more deeply explore the spiritual resources of our own and at the same time diminish the otherness of the other and create a more peaceable and just world in which all can find meaning in their all-too-human lives.

ABOUT THIS VOLUME

Against this background we may turn more directly to the fifth offering in the Dimensions of Asian Spirituality series, Sallie B. King's *Socially Engaged Buddhism*. Readers will, I believe, find inspiring the many and varied activities being undertaken throughout the world today by Buddhists struggling for justice both nationally and internationally—from the forests of Thailand to Zen centers in California, from the Sri Lankan countryside to the streets of New York, and almost everywhere in between.

This geographic breadth may come as a surprise to some who tend to place Buddhism almost solely in Asia. It has, however, always been a universalist religion not tied closely to any particular culture, as can be seen by how easily it became sinicized after leaving its South Asian birthplace while yet remaining distinctively Buddhist. The same may be said for the "transmission of the Dharma" to Tibet and Laos, to Sri Lanka and Japan, and, over the course of the past century—especially since the end of World War II—to the United States and Europe as well.

While Buddhists have been involved in the societies that nurtured them since the time of the Buddha himself, the now common expression "engaged Buddhism" is only somewhat misleading, for the faith began its highly activist phase worldwide only about half a century ago, in response to the manifold horrors visited on Asians then. In her introduction King catalogs "the multiple crises that hit Asia in the twentieth century. . . . Large parts of World War II, the Cold War, and the Vietnam War/war in Southeast Asia were fought there, directly affecting Japan, Korea, Vietnam, and much of the rest of Southeast Asia and resulting in millions of deaths." She then goes on to note genocide (Cambodia), great poverty and political uprootedness (Sri Lanka), deforestation (Thailand), and oppressive governments (Burma/Myanmar)—all this and more have befallen the Asian peoples in modern times, and had Buddhism not become engaged and activist, it would have become irrelevant in the cultures that nurtured it.

CHAPTER 1

Introduction

In the twentieth century, a politically and socially active form of Buddhism called Engaged Buddhism came into being and quickly became a large and powerful movement throughout Buddhist Asia; toward the end of that century, it also became very influential among Western Buddhists. In the Buddhist-majority countries of Asia, Engaged Buddhism became a vehicle capable of giving voice to the people's political aspirations and bringing down national governments. It became a path of psychological and practical liberation to oppressed peoples and of economic development to impoverished peoples. The reader may be surprised to hear of Buddhists engaging in this way with the problems of the world. It is true that the West has a considerably greater history of this kind of activism than Buddhist Asia. Nonetheless, Engaged Buddhism is a thoroughly Buddhist phenomenon.

What is Engaged Buddhism, and why did it emerge so dramatically in the twentieth century? Engaged Buddhism is a contemporary form of Buddhism that engages actively yet nonviolently with the social, economic, political, social, and ecological problems of society. At its best, this engagement is not separate from Buddhist spirituality, but is very much an expression of it.

Engaged Buddhism is not a centralized movement. It did not begin with the vision of a single charismatic leader and spread from there. Consequently, it is not defined by geography but is found wherever there are Buddhists with sufficient political freedom to engage with social and political issues as they see fit. It also is not defined by sect; Engaged Buddhism is neither a new Buddhist sect nor does it belong to one of the established sects. Theravada, Mahayana, Vajrayana, and nonsectarian Buddhists all may be involved with Engaged Buddhism, though not all Buddhists of any of these forms are Engaged Buddhists. Engaged Buddhism is defined and unified by the intention of Buddhists of whatever sect to apply the values and teachings of Buddhism to the problems of society in a nonviolent way, motivated by concern for the welfare of others and as an expression of their own Buddhist practices. With this kind of profile, there are no absolute lines defining who is and who is not an Engaged Buddhist. Some individuals and groups clearly belong at the core of this movement, such as Thich Nhat Hanh and Sarvodaya Shramadana, and others are borderline, such as groups and individuals that conscientiously put loving-kindness at the center of their practice but avoid societal or institutional engagement. We will focus in this book on groups and individuals that are at the core of the movement.

Engaged Buddhism came into being in the form of many individual movements in the various Asian Buddhist countries as a response to particular social, economic, political, and ecological crises facing each country. Its philosophical and ethical roots lie deeply within traditional Buddhist philosophy and values, which it applies to contemporary problems. This is the source of the unity evident among the Engaged Buddhists despite their dispersed and multiple origins throughout Buddhist Asia. However, Engaged Buddhism is also a modern phenomenon and as such has been influenced by modern social, economic, psychological, and political forms of analysis of Western origin. It has also been strongly influenced by the great example of Mahatma Gandhi, who pioneered spiritually based, nonviolent social engagement for the entire world.

The multiple crises that hit Asia in the twentieth century were devastating to much of Buddhist Asia. Large parts of World War II, the Cold War, and the Vietnam War/war in Southeast Asia were fought there, directly affecting Japan, Korea, Vietnam, and much of the rest of Southeast Asia and resulting in millions of deaths. There has been genocide in Cambodia and foreign invasion and cultural genocide in Tibet, again resulting in millions of deaths in both countries. Countries such as Sri Lanka have been impoverished and politically uprooted by colonial occupiers. Buddhist Asia has generated some extremely repressive governments—for example, Burma/Myanmar. Ecological crisis has become quite acute in some areas, such as Thailand, where deforestation has devastated some of the fishing and agricultural foundations of the economy.

Buddhist Asia has also seen some long-term social ills come to a head in the twentieth century, owing in part to the encounter with Western cultures—notably the extreme social inequality, bigotry, and poverty suffered by the ex-untouchables in India and the repressed and inferior status of women in much of Buddhist Asia. Finally, in the latter half of the twentieth century, Buddhist Asia was subjected to the powerful and related forces of rapid modernization, Westernization, and globalization, transforming foundational cultural patterns that have existed for centuries and even millennia.

It should be clear that if Buddhism had nothing to say about and did nothing in response to crises, challenges, and problems of this magnitude, it would have become so irrelevant to the lives of the people that it would have had little excuse for existing, other than perhaps to patch up people's psychological and spiritual wounds and send them back out into the fray. It simply was necessary for it to respond somehow. Fortunately a generation of creative, charismatic, and courageous leaders emerged throughout Buddhist Asia in the latter half of the twentieth century, responding to these crises in ways that were new and yet resonant with tradition.

Not every activist engagement of Buddhism with social and political issues can be considered Engaged Buddhism, however. Certainly the chauvinist Buddhist nationalism of contemporary Sri Lanka is not Engaged Buddhism inasmuch as its stance is based upon opposition and ill will toward the other—in this case, non-Buddhist Sri Lankan minorities—a stance that easily escalates into acts of violence, as has frequently occurred in recent decades. Engaged Buddhism is by definition nonviolent. It is also by definition an effort to express the *ideals* of Buddhism—including loving-kindness or universal goodwill toward *all*—in practical action, and on this point as well, nationalistic and chauvinistic Buddhism cannot be considered to be Engaged Buddhism; it is indeed the antithesis of it.

There are many Engaged Buddhist leaders and movements throughout Buddhist Asia and in the West today. The Buddhist teachers that are best known and most beloved in the West are two Engaged Buddhists: the Dalai Lama and Thich Nhat Hanh. They are both good examples of the characteristic nonviolence of Engaged Buddhism, even in the face of the greatest provocations: foreign invasion and war. Tenzin Gyatso, the Fourteenth Dalai Lama, is the spiritual leader of the Tibetan people and head of the Tibetan Liberation Movement, which struggles nonviolently for Tibetan self-determination. He fled Tibet in 1959, following the Chinese invasion and occupation of his country. Since that time he has lived in exile in Dharamsala, India, where he has prompted and overseen the transformation of the Tibetan government (now the Tibetan government in exile) from a medieval institution into a modern democracy. Despite the "worst case scenario" of foreign invasion and occupation and although his peace proposals to the Chinese have fallen on deaf ears, the Dalai Lama remains staunchly committed to a nonviolent approach to resolving Tibet's problems. With his engaging personality, good cheer, steadfast adherence to his ideals, and globe-trotting habits, he is almost universally known and admired and is the very face of Buddhism to most non-Buddhists. The Dalai Lama won the Nobel Peace Prize in 1989.

Thich Nhat Hanh is the Vietnamese Zen Buddhist monk and poet who was the most important ideological leader of the Vietnamese "Struggle Movement," which strove to bring an end to the war in Vietnam. Trained in Theravada as well as Zen, Thich Nhat Hanh coined the term "Engaged Buddhism," using it to refer to the kind of Buddhism that he wanted to see develop: one that would translate the wisdom and compassion that Buddhists strive to develop into concrete action on behalf of all sentient beings (that is, all beings with awareness, principally humans and animals). He cofounded the School of Youth for Social Service to train young Buddhists to serve the needs of the Vietnamese people, particularly in the countryside. During the war, he worked for peace by advocating a "Third Way," siding not with the North, not with the South, not against anyone, but with the people and with life. Since the war, he has lived in exile in France, unable to return to Vietnam for a visit until 2005. Nhat Hanh is one of the most important leaders creating and articulating Buddhist spiritual social activism, speaking to a global audience of Buddhists and non-Buddhists and frequently leading workshops all over the world for meditators, activists, families, veterans, artists, and therapists.

These leaders, while well known in the West, are but the tip of the iceberg of Asian Buddhist sociopolitical engagement, which is constituted not only of charismatic leaders but of millions of ordinary Buddhists as well. In every Buddhist country with sufficient political freedom, Asian Buddhists have responded to the crises facing their countries in creative ways. The Sarvodaya Shramadana, founded and headed by Dr. A. T. Ariyaratne, is the largest nongovernment organization in Sri Lanka. Ariyaratne pioneered the invention of "Buddhist economics" as an alternative to both capitalist and Communist economics, trying to build a society in which all needs are met—not only the economic, but social, cultural, psychological, political, and spiritual needs as well. Over half the villages of Sri Lanka have invited Sarvodaya to assist them to organize self-help economic development programs. In recent years, Sarvodaya has turned more and more of its attention to working for peace and reconciliation between the Sinhalese and Tamil populations.

In Cambodia, Somdech Preah Maha Ghosananda, sometimes called the Gandhi of Cambodia, was an important leader for peace and reconciliation. Fortuitously out of the country training in Thailand during the Khmer Rouge era, Maha Ghosananda was one of the few Cambodian monks to survive that era. He led the restoration of Buddhism after the Khmer Rouge had all but wiped it out, and as head of Cambodian Buddhism, he worked hard to heal the profound wounds of the Cambodian people, both at home and abroad. He created the annual Dhammayietra, or Peace Walk, which accompanied refugees returning home from the camps, and in subsequent years he drew significant attention and engagement to remaining areas of conflict. He was one of the major leaders of the international movement to ban land mines. Despite the fact that his entire family died during the Cambodian Holocaust, he always radiated infectious joy. He died in 2007.

In Thailand a number of "development monks" pioneer ways to help impoverished villagers, such as by providing loans for seed from donations made to the temples. "Ecology monks" work to protect the highly endangered environment, with particular concern for loss of land to deforestation and dams. Such work can challenge vested interests and is therefore dangerous; it can expose the monks to charges of political activity unbefitting a monk, with defrocking occasionally following as a consequence.

In Burma, also known as Myanmar, laywoman and Nobel Peace Prize laureate Aung San Suu Kyi leads the movement for democracy and human rights. Her party, the National League for Democracy, has worked since 1988 to bring an end to the brutal military regime ruling Burma and institute civilian democratic government. In the summer of 1988 the streets of Rangoon (now Yangon) were filled with students and Buddhist monks calling for an end to the military government and the institution of human rights. When her party won a landslide electoral victory in 1990, Aung San Suu Kyi was placed under house arrest, where she has been kept most of the time since. Whenever she is released, she resumes political activity, and after a time she is once again placed under house arrest. She is under house arrest at this writing. Monks and students demonstrated in the streets of Burma again in 2007.

Based in Taiwan, the nun Venerable Cheng Yen is the founder of Tzu Chi, a huge charitable organization with over four million members in Taiwan and abroad. Tzu Chi's most important contributions have been the establishment of free medical care, in Taiwan and elsewhere; the establishment of the world's third largest bone marrow data bank; and the provision of international emergency relief. Unlike other Engaged Buddhist groups, Tzu Chi has a policy of remaining strictly unengaged in political issues. This has allowed it entrée to the People's Republic of China and North Korea, where its offers of emergency aid have been welcomed in times of natural disasters.

There are many other Engaged Buddhist leaders and movements throughout Asia. Many of these movements involve hundreds of thousands or even millions of active participants. While Engaged Buddhism can sometimes be controversial simply because it challenges tradition by working in innovative ways, it is by no means a fringe movement. Many of the best educated, most idealistic and progressive monastics and laypeople are its leaders, thinkers, activists, and participants. There are certainly conservative and reactionary groups in the Buddhist world, but the liberal and progressive Engaged Buddhist movement very much holds its own against them.

In the West, because Buddhism is much smaller, Engaged Buddhism is also much smaller. But Westerners likewise are proving very attracted to Engaged Buddhism and very adaptive in developing new expressions of it. To name just a few examples, Western Engaged Buddhists work to end capital punishment; guard nuclear wastes; challenge racism, sexism, and militarism; and protect the lives and well-being of animals. American Zen master and Engaged Buddhist leader Bernie Glassman, one of the most creative of the Western Engaged Buddhist leaders, founded the Zen Peacemaker Order, with such programs as "street retreats," in which the affluent make a spiritual retreat by living on the streets of New York; pilgrimages to Auschwitz-Birkenau, where the retreatants bear witness to the events of the Holocaust and sit with minds and hearts open to insight and transformation; the Greyston Mandala, a network of social and economic development programs focusing on self-help employment and housing for formerly homeless and poor people; and housing and health services for people with HIV/AIDS. Laywoman and environmental activist Joanna Macy has created "despair and empowerment" workshops to help both activists and ordinary people overwhelmed by their concern for the present shape of the world. She created the nuclear guardianship project to help us face up to the responsibilities inherent in creating nuclear wastes, which remain dangerous for millennia. Glassman and Macy are just two examples of the more creative of the Engaged Buddhist leaders in the West, but there are many more and thousands more ordinary practitioners who look for ways to express their Engaged Buddhist values through their occupations—perhaps by choosing a service profession as a means of livelihood or by trying to make their workplace more humane and peaceful—or in political or environmental activism.

This brief overview of the history and scope of Engaged Buddhism has perhaps left the reader with a nagging question: Why are Buddhists engaging with the social and political problems of the world? The terrible crises of the twentieth century have been named as the major reason for engagement, but surely there have been terrible times in the past, in the long history (two and a half millennia) of Buddhism. Is it not contrary to well-established Buddhist habits to engage with the problems of samsara (the world of birth, death, rebirth, and redeath)? Doesn't the Buddha teach that we should practice nonattachment from worldly things?

Here we open up what is controversial about Engaged Buddhism among more traditional and conservative Buddhists in Asia, many of whom argue exactly this point. Perhaps all of their lives they have thought of the bhikkhus (monks) as "fields of merit," the means by which laypeople may earn merit, or good karma. This view is based upon the idea that giving is a meritorious act and therefore earns the giver good karma. The purer the recipient of the gift, it is believed, the more merit one's gift earns. Since the bhikkhus practice a considerably more exacting self-discipline than laypeople, the bhikkhu is widely believed to be the purest, or best, object of giving for the purpose of earning merit. Many laypeople, especially in Southeast Asia, want their bhikkhus to stay in the temples, where they will be "pure" and thus more fit as recipients of their *dāna* (giving). They can be rather dismayed when they see their bhikkhus out helping to dig a road with Sarvodaya Shramadana or carrying a briefcase off to a meeting with a government official. In the West, some Buddhist scholars argue that since engagement with the problems of the world is a Western habit, Engaged Buddhism, which developed in the twentieth century just when Westernization was overwhelming Asia, is simply Westernized Buddhism and hence distorted Buddhism. In this way, Engaged Buddhism is sometimes criticized by both Asians and Westerners.

In response to the question "Why engagement?" Thich Nhat Hanh has a simple answer: Buddhism has always been engaged. All of Buddhism is engaged because all of it addresses human suffering. That is true. Siddhartha Gautama does not fully become the Buddha when he experiences enlightenment sitting beneath the Bo tree; the wisdom gained beneath the Bo tree is only the first of the two defining characteristics of a Buddha. Gautama fully becomes the Buddha when he turns back toward humankind within samsara and begins to teach, demonstrating his compassion—the second defining characteristic of a Buddha—specifically his compassion for sentient beings suffering within samsara. A Buddha is distinguished in tradition from a *pratyekabuddha*, a "solitary" Buddha who, like Gautama, is enlightened on his own but, unlike Gautama, does not teach humankind. A *pratyekabuddha*, while recognized by Buddhism as a spiritual possibility, is on a different path from that followed by the founder of Buddhism. Therefore, inasmuch as Buddhism is founded not only in Gautama's enlightenment but also in his decision to teach, it is fair to say that it has always been engaged, always focused on the problem of *duḥkha* (Pali, *dukkha,* loosely translated as "suffering") and the overcoming of *duḥkha.*

A. T. Ariyaratne also answers the question "Why engagement?" by arguing that Buddhism has always been engaged, but he takes a different approach, also well founded. Ariyaratne points out that before the advent of colonialism, Buddhism was very much engaged with secular matters in society; it was the colonial occupation, he argues, that drove Buddhism away from this engagement. It is true that one can find secular matters discussed in the Buddhist scriptures in considerable detail. The Buddha taught about proper and considerate behavior within the family and with teachers, friends, and acquaintances of all kinds; he gave teachings on financial matters, such as how much money to save and how much to invest in business; he gave teachings on ethical and unethical ways of earning a livelihood; he gave teachings on proper behavior for rulers; he personally advised rulers and intervened to try to stop a war; he personally nursed a sick disciple and urged his followers to learn medicine. In addition, throughout Southeast Asia in the premodern period, one typically found a Buddhist temple in every village of any size. The bhikkhus of such a temple performed many secular functions—they taught children the rudiments of literacy and math, attended to the villagers' medical needs, advised the village elders from a nonpartisan perspective, and counseled individuals—in addition to their more religious functions of teaching the Dharma, setting a moral example, and providing the villagers the opportunity to give and earn merit. In the capital, bhikkhus often served as advisers to the rulers. One can hardly look at these examples and conclude that Buddhism was not engaged with worldly matters.

Ariyaratne points out that in Sri Lanka all of this changed when the British took control. The British brought in Western education, so the bhikkhus were less needed as teachers; they brought in Western medicine, so the bhikkhus were less needed as medical consultants. Clearly the bhikkhus were not wanted as advisers to the British rulers. Thus the more secular functions of the bhikkhus were steadily and intentionally eroded, allowing the Christian missionaries who came with the British rulers to criticize Buddhism as being unconcerned with the mundane welfare of the people! To this day, Sri Lankan Christians continue to rebuke Buddhism for being otherworldly and unconcerned with the welfare of the people; in one generation, the true historical perspective has been forgotten.

For historical accuracy, we must qualify these statements that Buddhism has always been engaged, never disengaged. The matter is more complex. While it is true that in Southeast Asia one could find a Buddhist temple in every village, there have always been both village and forest-dwelling bhikkhus within traditional Buddhism. The village bhikkhu was engaged with the villagers as teacher, doctor, adviser. However, there was also the hermit, the forest-dwelling bhikkhu who intentionally withdrew from society and village life—at least for a time, maybe for a lifetime—in order to focus on intensive meditation practice, with the goal of attaining enlightenment and nirvana. In other regions of Asia, some bhikkhus, and sometimes laymen, also took up the more eremitic option, seeking out caves or building huts in the mountains for the same purpose of intentionally cutting themselves off from society in order to focus exclusively on practice. Clearly Buddhism can and does accommodate those whose spirituality leads them to withdraw from society, though this has always remained a minority option, an important point to bear in mind. The Dalai Lama notes that very few people possess the vocation of the forest (cave, mountain) dweller; it is right, he says, for only a handful. Very few people will flourish if they take themselves away from human society. The village-dwelling monastics, as well as the vast majority of laypeople, are pulled by their very practice and the loving-kindness and compassion that it engenders to help in whatever way they can. For them, Engaged

Buddhism, which asks only that loving-kindness and compassion be expressed in a concrete way, is a natural fit.

As for the charge that Engaged Buddhism is Westernized Buddhism, it must be recognized that there has been considerable Western influence on its leadership. Dr. B. R. Ambedkar received an extensive Western education. Aung San Suu Kyi was married to an Englishman (until he died) and lived for decades in the West. Thich Nhat Hanh spent some formative years in the West and received some education there. Most of the Engaged Buddhist leaders are in regular touch with the Western world and travel in the West frequently. Western ways of thinking do turn up in Engaged Buddhism, such as in the ideas of structural violence and institutionalized poverty. This does not mean, however, that Engaged Buddhism is Westernized Buddhism in the sense that it is the product of Western influences.

Generally, one finds that Engaged Buddhism is based in a Buddhist worldview and builds its ideas primarily from traditional Buddhist philosophy, ethics, and spirituality. Engaged Buddhist leaders interpret these ideas with a concern to *apply* them to the problems facing their societies today, motivated by the traditional Buddhist virtue of compassion. The greatest influence from non-Buddhists comes from Gandhi (himself Western educated), who has exerted a great influence on the Engaged Buddhist leaders, with the exception of Dr. Ambedkar (who worked with Gandhi but eventually broke with him owing to Gandhi's refusal to reject the caste system). Western influence comes from the example of Christian charitable work and activism and elements of Western analysis drawn from the social sciences, particularly sociology, economics, and political science.

Two important points must be understood with respect to Western influences on Engaged Buddhism. The first is that the Engaged Buddhist leaders have not been passive recipients of Western ideas and practices. They have embraced Western ideas that they have found useful, such as human rights, and largely left alone those that they have not found compatible with their Buddhist worldview, such as the idea of political justice. They also sometimes challenge Western ideas and practices, such as the anger in anti-war protests during the Vietnam War or what they perceive as excessive individualism in Western societies.

The second point is that Engaged Buddhism has not been distorted by Western influence. I hope this book will demonstrate how thoroughly *Buddhist* Engaged Buddhism is. Everything the Engaged Buddhists say and do can be, and is, justified on the basis of traditional Buddhist views and values. Most convincingly, all the projects and actions are permeated with Buddhist spirituality in such a way that they are subtly, or not so subtly, different from similar projects and actions in the West. Work for national or international peace is presented as inseparable from the cultivation of inner peace. Work to eliminate poverty is seen as interdependent with efforts to cultivate spirituality and protect the environment. To engage in social work requires profound adjustment in the sense of "self" and "other." Environmental work weakens the feeling of separation between oneself and the natural world.

It is then primarily a *Buddhist* intellectual and spiritual world that the Engaged Buddhists inhabit. It is also, however, a *modern* world. All religions change over time; the Asian Engaged Buddhists are important modernizers of Buddhism, adapting tradition to contemporary challenges, as has been done in every religion around the world time and again. The Engaged Buddhist world is, finally, a *globalized* world. We live in a time in which the world is shrinking, as news and ideas instantly circle the globe electronically; people, products, and pollution travel with small attention to national boundaries; and cultures and societies become ever more tightly knit together. In such a triple world, the Engaged Buddhists skillfully balance their roles as transmitters of traditions and values, transformers of tradition, and negotiators of tradition in a world in which the old boundaries are falling down.

CHAPTER 2

Philosophy and Ethics

As we have seen, Engaged Buddhism is a noncentralized movement that emerged in response to multiple crises in modern Asia. The leaders and groups that make up the movement all draw upon traditional Buddhist concepts, values, and principles as they develop their various responses to the crises and challenges of their particular situations. It is this shared grounding in traditional Buddhism that ties together the various Engaged Buddhist groups. Let us examine some of these foundational teachings and the ways in which they shape Engaged Buddhism.

Key Concepts

KARMA, CAUSALITY, DEPENDENT ORIGINATION, AND INTERDEPENDENCE

"Karma" means "action." More broadly, it refers to the law of cause and effect, a natural law of the cosmos, as it applies to human actions in the forms of thoughts, words, and deeds. People who engage in negatively motivated acts, thoughts, or speech—that is, deeds motivated by greed, hatred, or delusion—reap negative results in this life or a future life; similarly, positively motivated acts, such as those motivated by generosity, loving-kindness, or moral self-discipline, bring positive results. Metaphorically one's actions "sow" karmic "seeds," which gestate for a short or a long time, eventuating in karmic results or "fruit."

Karma is part of the foundational Buddhist teaching of causality or conditionality, expressed in Buddhist thought as dependent origination. According to this teaching, all things come into being as a result of other things—that is, all things are interdependent. As the Buddha put it, "When this exists, that comes to be; with the arising of this, that arises. When this does not exist, that does not come to be; with the cessation of this, that ceases." This pattern applies to all things—human and natural, individual and social, psychological and physical. This may seem to be a bit of rather abstract philosophy, but the teachings of the Buddha are very practical. There is a tremendous liberating potential, a power, that derives from the understanding that everything in the world operates in terms of cause and effect. Dependent origination is a key teaching for spirituality because it means that if there is something unwholesome from which one wants to be free (such as craving, aversion, or delusion—the "three poisons" that make samsaric experience what it is), then one should look to the causes and conditions that bring that reality into being and see what action can be brought to bear to eliminate or alter those causes or conditions.

The Engaged Buddhists often emphasize this practicality of the Buddha's teachings. While the usefulness of the teaching of dependent origination has traditionally been applied to personal spiritual transformation, the Engaged Buddhists see no reason not to apply it to societal transformation as well. Thus if there is something unwholesome from which one wants to free the world (for example, war, poverty, racism), then one should look to the causes and conditions that bring that reality into being and see what action can be brought to bear to eliminate or alter those causes or conditions. The Engaged Buddhists often take this approach in their work.

THE FOUR NOBLE TRUTHS

Thinking in terms of causality and karma is one of the keys to all Buddhist efforts, whether spiritual or socially engaged. Another key is the Four Noble Truths. The Four Noble Truths are the basic framework of the Buddha's spiritual teachings, which point the way to liberation by way of the radical transformation of the manner of human being, the way in which humans "are." Like the teachings on dependent origination, the Four Noble Truths are preeminently practical teachings, meant to be used for the liberation of humankind.

The First Noble Truth is *duḥkha* (Pali, *dukkha*). The standard English translation of *duḥkha* is "suffering"; however, this translation is misleading in some respects. Fundamentally *duḥkha* is the nonfit between what humans want (unending pleasure and security) and what conditioned existence gives us (a mix of pleasure and pain, plus constant change where we look for some unchanging certainties upon which to base our security). Certainly *duḥkha* includes all mundane suffering (illness, hunger, fear, and physical and mental pain), but it also goes beyond it to include the fundamental human dis-ease: our inability to be satisfied with life, our constant craving for more and better. All of this was pointed out as a simple fact by the Buddha, without negative judgment; it is simply the way we are. Since we are the way we are and life is the way it is, we are bound to be dissatisfied. This does not mean that we are always suffering; this is simply untrue. It means that even our pleasure is *duḥkha* since it always passes, and even if it remained, we would become bored with it and want something better. This is the human condition. *Duḥkha,* the human dis-ease with the human condition, states the problem that Buddhism is dedicated to solving. The Buddha is the Great Physician, who shows the way to cure the human dis-ease.

The Second Noble Truth states the cause of *duḥkha.* Here again Buddhism is very practical, as well as rational. If one has a problem and wants to fully resolve it—as opposed to denying it, averting one's eyes from it, distracting one's mind from it, or putting a Band-Aid on it—then one needs to identify the root cause of that problem and do something about that cause. The Buddha named craving (always wanting something) and ignorance (specifically, our fundamental ignorance about who and what we are, our mistaken belief that the word "I" refers to a real entity that constitutes our identity) as the root causes of *duḥkha.* Here thinking in terms of dependent origination impinges on the Four Noble Truths. As the Buddha said, "When this does not exist, that does not come to be." If we could rid ourselves of craving and ignorance (no easy task, of course!), *duḥkha* would not come to be.

The Third Noble Truth, nirvana or enlightenment, states the goal in both a negative and a positive form. The negative form is the Buddha's assurance that *duḥkha* can be eradicated at its roots; we can rid ourselves of what we don't want. The Third Noble Truth is also, in a more positive sense, the Buddha's assurance that one's own nature can be radically transformed, such that one's daily life experience will be constituted of wisdom and compassion. This is a positive goal for which one is reaching.

The Buddha famously refused to say very much at all about nirvana. Nirvana, he made it clear, is known experientially and cannot be correctly expressed in words. But since language can tell us what nirvana is *not,* it can at least point us in the right direction. Nirvana is the contrary of samsara. Where samsara is delusion and ignorance, nirvana must be freedom from those conditions—that is, enlightenment and wisdom. Where samsara is karmic bondage, nirvana is liberation. Where samsara is characterized by *duḥkha,* nirvana is blissful freedom from *duḥkha.* But since all of our language is based upon samsaric experience and samsaric experience is by definition the contrary of nirvanic experience, whatever one might attempt to say of nirvana using samsaric language would not only be false, but also, more seriously, would make us think that we knew something about nirvana when in fact we did not. This false belief about nirvana would constitute an active barrier in our mind, making it more difficult to attain experiential knowledge of the true nature of nirvana.

To illustrate what I mean, consider Michelangelo's painting on the ceiling of the Sistine Chapel. In it he depicts God as an old man with a long white beard up in the sky. Most adults recognize that God, if he exists (which Buddhists deny), is not an old man with a long white beard up in the sky. Nevertheless, that image takes up a tremendous amount of space in the minds of those of us raised in Western culture and is very hard to shake. It actively gets in the way of a more mature understanding of the nature of God. Now Buddhists deny the existence of God, so this is not a problem for them. But if the Buddha had given teachings that articulated, as best he could, the nature of nirvana, those teachings would have become a similar kind of obstacle. Recognizing the nature of verbal thought (thinking in words) as an obstacle for experiential knowledge of nirvana, out of compassion for humankind and in the hope that we would eventually attain experiential knowledge of our own, the Buddha refrained from speaking of nirvana or spoke of it with negative words. Unfortunately many people have misunderstood the Buddha's teachings and wrongly believe that the goal of nirvana is a goal of absolute extinction, whereas it is the extinction only of samsaric experience, of karmic bondage, ignorance, and *duḥkha*. The Buddha refused to fill out the picture of what nirvana is in a positive sense, but he did assure us that it is possible for us to attain it.

Here is where Buddhism becomes a religion and the Buddhist version of faith enters the picture. The Buddha never asked anyone to believe anything on his authority. On the contrary, he urged people to look into everything they were told, including the teachings of the multiple religious teachers circulating in India at the time; to observe their own lives and minds; and to believe something only when they were convinced of it on the basis of their own personal experiential knowledge. So there should be no blind faith in Buddhism. At the same time, in order to practice Buddhism, one does have to trust that the Buddha probably knew what he was talking about. After all, the practice of Buddhism requires quite a lot of effort over an extended period of time. One is not going to make such a sustained effort unless one believes that it is probably going to be worthwhile. The Third Noble Truth works like this: Until one has experienced it, one does not know for sure the reality of nirvana or enlightenment, in an experiential sense. However, in order to practice Buddhism one must feel that it is probable that the practice will yield results. Buddhist thinking on this subject has evolved over time and varies from one Buddhist sect to another, but generally most Buddhists today believe that enlightenment comes in degrees, and few expect to manifest complete enlightenment anytime soon, though they do hope to see in themselves some gradually diminishing egotism, growing compassion, and deepening wisdom (perhaps marked by a few sudden flashes of insight). The point of the Third Noble Truth is that there is hope that people can transform themselves, that we are not doomed to experiencing unending *duḥkha*.

With the Fourth Noble Truth, the path, Buddhist practicality becomes concrete. If one wants to achieve the goal held out for us in the Third Noble Truth, then the Fourth Noble Truth offers a set of practices with which to do so. The path, as taught by the Buddha, is the Noble Eightfold Path, the path to the eradication of *duḥkha*. Made up of eight components, its practices fall into the three categories of moral self-discipline, mental self-discipline, and wisdom. Moral self-discipline, the most basic set of practices, includes Right Speech, Right Action, and Right Livelihood. Mental self-discipline includes Right Effort, Right Mindfulness, and Right Concentration. Wisdom is constituted of Right Understanding and Right Thought. These are not practices that one takes up one at a time in sequential fashion; rather, they are mutually supportive and interactive, and one practices them more or less simultaneously.

One major guidance that the Engaged Buddhists take from the Four Noble Truths is their focus on suffering. The First Noble Truth states the problem that Buddhism is designed to cure: *duḥkha*. The Buddha himself said, "I teach only *duḥkha* and the utter quenching of *duḥkha*." The Engaged Buddhists take this *duḥkha* to mean suffering of all kinds, spiritual and mundane, and take as their own goal the elimination of all kinds of suffering, including spiritual. They understand that where there is *duḥkha,* there is a problem; where there is no *duḥkha,* there is no problem.

The Four Noble Truths are also used by the Engaged Buddhists as a template for analysis. In this usage, the First Noble Truth states the problem, the second analyzes and identifies the cause of the problem, the third points to the goal that one hopes to reach, and the fourth details what one has to do to reach that goal.

HUMAN NATURE

In the Buddhist view, there is no human soul or fixed self. The word "I," which we believe refers to something that constitutes one's personal identity, is a fiction; there is no thing that is the core of one's identity. This is the Buddha's teaching of *anātman* (Pali, *anatta*), or no-self. This idea can be approached in three ways. First, we lack a self because as human beings, we are compound beings, made up of multiple physical and psychological processes and parts. Our bodies are constituted of multiple cells and organs, multiple respiratory, digestive, eliminative, and other processes. Our mental life is constituted of multiple thoughts, emotions, intentions, perceptions, sensations, and even multiple kinds of awareness (visual awareness, tactile awareness, auditory awareness, olfactory awareness, awareness of taste and awareness of thoughts). There is no single core, essence, or entity that can be found amidst this multiplicity of processes and parts that can be identified as constituting one's selfhood or the basis of one's identity, the "essence" of who one is.

Second, human beings lack a self because we are beings that are always in process, changing moment by moment. Our thoughts and emotions change rapidly, our skin cells slough continually off the surface of our skin, and even the cells of our bones change and are replaced over time. A self would have to endure at least throughout one's lifetime (or multiple lifetimes, in the Buddhist view), but there is no such thing that can be identified in the human being. In many ways, we are constantly constructing ourselves by the choices we make—the food we choose to eat, the friends with whom we choose to associate, the ideas to which we turn. Clearly these choices are not and cannot be made in isolation. They exist as part of the great web of interdependence. Thus each one of us comes into being and is constructed not only by and through our parents, but also through the causal and conditioning influences of the air we breathe, the Earth we stand upon, the food we eat, the love or abuse we receive from family, the ideas we learn from teachers, the images impressed upon our minds by media, the trust and suspicion we develop through peer relationships, the culture that gives us language and concepts, and so forth. We do not exist for a moment in isolation from all these things. We are like all other things in the world, being caused and conditioned by others and causing and conditioning others in turn. So, third, no-self is a function of interdependence; we are not sufficiently separate from the "other" beings and things around us to be correctly understood as separate selves.

In Buddhism the philosophical idea of no-self is closely connected to the spiritual value of selflessness. They are two sides of a single coin. One who understands that there is no self should be free of egotism and self-centeredness in his or her attitudes and behavior. One who has an intellectual understanding of no-self but still behaves in an egotistical manner has no real insight or experiential understanding of it—that is, no real understanding at all. Freedom from egotism is

probably the single most important measure that the ordinary Buddhist uses in deciding whether a Buddhist teacher knows what she or
he is talking about and is therefore worth listening to.

We saw in the discussion of the Second Noble Truth that human
craving—our incessantly wanting more and better—and ignorance—
our fundamental and specific ignorance about who and what we are,
a gut-level belief that "I" am a separate self—are named as the root
causes of *duḥkha,* our dissatisfaction with life. Craving and ignorance
are inherently interconnected as "I want." Together they are the very
foundation of ordinary human psychology, the "I want" this and "I
don't want" that, that drive us through our days and leave us dissatisfied when our endless wants cannot all be fulfilled.

This incessant craving and ignorance about who and what we are
constitute the major factors in the Buddhist view that there is something fundamentally wrong in human nature. The Buddhist view of
human nature, however, is far from pessimistic. In addition to our fundamental craving and ignorance, we have another quality that is a fundamental part of human nature, this time positively so: *chanda*—the
basic urge that all humans have to better themselves, to grow spiritually,
to draw closer to goodness and truth. Because humans are not fixed
selves but are constantly changing beings, we can and do develop; we
are constantly becoming other-than-we-were. This is why the lack of a
self in human beings is actually a positive thing: if we were fixed selves,
we would not be changing, and change provides an opportunity for betterment. All of Buddhism is based upon the fact that human beings are
beings in process, changing and developing beings. Change can be for
either better or worse. Buddhism is a system that supplies wholesome
causes and conditions to this process of human change so that we can
maximize our opportunity for development in a positive direction.

THIS PRECIOUS HUMAN LIFE:
HUMAN ENLIGHTENABILITY AND BUDDHA NATURE

When they hear of the Buddhist teaching of no-self *(anātman/anatta)*,
many people wrongly conclude that human life is somehow devalued
in Buddhism. After all, they reason, if in the ultimate analysis there

is no real "self" or person there, why would one particularly concern oneself about "it"? Nothing could be farther from the truth. The teaching of no-self means only that there is no independent, unchanging metaphysical entity within a human being. There is, however, still a perfectly real set of interdependent events, experiences, thoughts, physical processes, and so forth that constitutes human being. Traditional Buddhism teaches that in the revolvings of samsaric existence, sentient beings may be born and reborn as gods, human beings, titans, hungry ghosts, animals, or hell beings, depending upon their karma. Out of these six forms of samsaric existence, all forms of Buddhism recognize the human birth as the precious birth because it is only as a human being that conditions are right for a sentient being to achieve enlightenment. The Buddha walked away from the Hindu caste system, which allowed only members of the upper social classes access to religious teachings, and taught "with an open hand" to anyone interested in hearing. He accepted disciples from all the social classes, women as well as men. He confirmed during his lifetime that people of all social classes and both sexes had attained enlightenment.

According to the Buddha, humans are able to attain enlightenment because we all possess the quality of *chanda*, the desire for our own betterment, for drawing closer to truth and goodness. Later in the history of Buddhism, Buddhists in India and China debated extensively whether all sentient beings, sooner or later, would achieve enlightenment or whether some would simply never be able to do so. Though both sides of the question were argued, the schools that held that some would never be able to achieve enlightenment died out. The Mahayana Buddhism that spread throughout North and East Asia takes as one of its central tenets that "all sentient beings possess the Buddha nature." There are two readings of this teaching, both of which are embraced. First, since we all possess the Buddha nature, we all possess an embryonic Buddha within. Because of this, we have the potential to achieve Buddhahood, the perfection of wisdom and compassion, once we develop that seed of Buddhahood, and will do so in time. In the second reading, since we all possess the Buddha nature, we all already *are* Buddhas, but we don't experience ourselves (or others) that way because our Buddhahood is concealed from us by our delusion. Once we can break through that delusion, we will realize that we always have been Buddhas, perfectly enlightened and compassionate beings.

Thus the Buddhist view of human being, though it does deny the existence of an independent, entitative self, strongly affirms the value and preciousness of each human life. In Buddhist countries, this view is an important foundation of Buddhist arguments for human rights, as we shall see in chapter 6. By denying the entitative self and emphasizing interdependence, this view does, however, tend to discourage the formation of the kind of strongly individualistic society that is common in the West (especially the United States) and encourage a more communitarian society, with a relatively stronger emphasis on the importance of social groups and on the natural world. It is less forgetful of the fact that the individual does not stand alone but is very much formed by society and the physical world.

Buddhist Ethics

Turning to Buddhist ethics, we may begin by considering some basic values of Buddhism: compassion, loving-kindness, giving, the five lay precepts, and nonviolence.

COMPASSION, LOVING-KINDNESS, GIVING, AND THE BODHISATTVA

Compassion *(karuṇā)* is one of two defining characteristics of a Buddha, the other being wisdom. Siddhartha Gautama required two things to become the Buddha: the experience of enlightenment beneath the Bo tree *and* the decision to teach sentient beings, out of compassion for their suffering. As such, compassion represents a good part of the transformed state for which Buddhists strive, and for this reason it stands out among the long list of esteemed virtues in Buddhism, especially in the Mahayana tradition. Compassion specifically means caring about the suffering or *duḥkha* of others.

Compassion and loving-kindness are closely related virtues, representing two facets of benevolence, or goodwill. Though both the Theravada and Mahayana traditions embrace both values, the former tends to speak more frequently of loving-kindness while the latter emphasizes compassion. Loving-kindness (*maitri/mettā;* one tends to see the latter, Pali, term more frequently) means universal beneficence or goodwill—that is, wishing for the happiness and well-being of others. It is a close companion of compassion, though the tone of compassion is negative (hoping that others will *not* suffer) while the tone of loving-kindness is positive (hoping that others *will* be happy). Both of these values are closely tied to the development of freedom from selfishness and ego-centeredness—as one actively cares more about the welfare of others, one is focusing less and less upon oneself. Traditionally in many Buddhist countries the layperson, who had little time for meditation and the study of Buddhist texts, focused upon the development of loving-kindness and compassion and the translation of these values into action through the virtue of giving.

Giving or generosity *(dāna)* is a basic value of the layperson but is also important in the monastic's life. In Southeast Asia in particular the monastics rely directly upon the laypeople for meeting their material needs. Traditionally laypeople have been eager to give material necessities to the ordained monastics as it has been believed (as noted in chapter 1) that the greater the merit of the one to whom one gives, the greater the merit, or good karma, earned by the giver. Thus the laypeople have by no means seen this relationship as a burden; on the contrary, they see the monastics as "fields of merit," a boon in the form of an opportunity to earn merit. In return, the monastics give their teachings of the Dharma, their counsel, the example of their self-discipline and aspiration, and such practical help as medical care and elementary secular teaching. While giving to the monastics has traditionally been emphasized, it has always been important to give to others as well—to family, guests, teachers, the needy, travelers, and others. In some countries it was the custom to leave water out by the side of the road for any passerby who might want to drink it. Others planted trees by the side of the road to provide shade. One should never leave a needy person in want. In addition, one should give nonmaterial goods: one's time, attention, moral support, labor, and the like.

In the Mahayana tradition, when one cares enough about sentient beings' suffering, one will be moved to vow to return again and again to samsara as a bodhisattva to help all sentient beings become free of suffering. This is the arising of *bodhicitta,* the "thought of enlighten-ment," a definitive stage in one's spiritual development on the path to enlightenment. Bodhisattvas fall into two categories. There are the great celestial bodhisattvas, who represent the perfection of various virtues and for whose help the ordinary person can ask. Avalokites-vara (Tibetan, Chenrezig; Chinese, Kuan-yin; Japanese, Kannon), the Bodhisattva of Compassion, for example, is the most beloved bodhi-sattva throughout East Asia. With his or her (there are both male and female forms) many eyes looking for beings in need and hands ready to take action, Avalokitesvara is believed to assist anyone who cries out for help. A subtler, but traditional, understanding recognizes that there is no absolute line between the bodhisattvas and us. Thus one may meditate on Avalokitesvara (who ultimately is an aspect of one's own mind) in order to help cultivate one's own compassion. The other kind of bodhisattva is any practitioner who has felt the arising of *bodhi-citta* and taken bodhisattva vows. Of course they are far inferior to the great celestial bodhisattvas in the development of their wisdom and compassion, yet they are on the same path. Thus Engaged Buddhist leader Venerable Cheng Yen can urge her followers to become Kuan-yin's watchful eyes and helpful hands by volunteering their service for the care of others.

THE FIVE PRECEPTS AND NONHARMFULNESS

The five lay precepts in many ways embody the basic moral code of Buddhism. They are five "training precepts" that cannot be com-manded—since there is no God in Buddhism to do the command-ing—but that one willingly takes upon oneself because one sees their value and inherent goodness. In observing the five precepts, one undertakes not to destroy life, steal, commit sexual misconduct, lie, or ingest intoxicants. We are encouraged to avoid these five acts because if we do them, we cause harm to ourselves and others; that is, we harm others directly if we kill them or steal from them, but we also cause ourselves harm because we earn very negative karma by committing such acts.

Nonviolence and nonharmfulness are rooted in the first lay pre-cept, the idea of karma, experiential understanding of no-self, and the values of compassion and loving-kindness, all of which come together in nonharmfulness. One avoids breaking the first precept if one avoids taking life, but this is only the beginning; the spirit of the first precept—and indeed all of Buddhism—invites one not only to avoid killing other living beings, but also to avoid harming them and, in fact, to nurture them. Any act of intentionally harming another living being earns negative karma. It is also an expression of egotism, the (usually subconscious) belief that "I" am more important than the being whom "I" harm, and, of course, it is the opposite of compassion and loving-kindness. Just as the ordinary Buddhist expects his teachers and leaders to be free of egotism, he also expects them to be free of violence in thought, word, and deed and to live, act, and speak gently, kindly, and benevolently.

These are the ideals. In practice, some Buddhist individuals and groups—including some contemporary activist individuals and groups—violate them with hateful, aggressive, and sometimes violent words and behavior. For example, some Sri Lankans are chauvinistic and nationalistic about Buddhism and want to define non-Buddhist Sri Lankans as second-class citizens at best. At worst, this Buddhism is both an expression of and a fuel for the ethnic hatred and civil war that beset that country. Another example is the famous Bhikkhu Kitthiwuttho of Thailand, who argued in the 1970s that "killing communists is not demeritorious"—that is, it earns the one who kills no bad karma. Such forms of Buddhism, which express contempt and ill will toward an Other, are the very antithesis of the teachings of the Buddha. Ultimately the implication of the doctrines of no-self and interdependence is that *there is no other*. Self and other, Tamil and Sinhalese, co-create each other. In past lives they have been each other. In the present they inhale and exhale the same air, taking it into their bloodstreams; they construct each other's thoughts with their words and deeds. The reification of the Other into a static category sealed off from one's own is contrary to the teachings of the Buddha; reality is a great web of interaction and mutual creation from which nothing and no one stands apart. Moreover, the Buddha taught—and later Buddhists extensively developed—the teaching that truth is to be found in experience, not in ideas, much less in ideologies. To cling to ideas of the Other that we

and I am the bird which, when spring comes,
    arrives in time to eat the mayfly. . . .

I am the 12-year-old girl, refugee
    on a small boat,
who throws herself into the ocean after
    being raped by a sea pirate,
and I am the pirate, my heart not yet capable
    of seeing and loving. . . .

My joy is like spring, so warm it makes
    flowers bloom in all walks of life.
My pain is like a river of tears, so full it
    fills up the four oceans.

Please call me by my true names,
so I can hear all my cries and my laughs
    at once,
so I can see that my joy and pain are one.

Please call me by my true names,
    so I can wake up,
and so the door of my heart can be left open,
the door of compassion.

This poem can be quite shocking upon a first reading. The parallel setup between the bird and the rapist may seem to condone the rapist—after all, we don't judge a bird that is eating an insect as morally reprehensible, and Nhat Hanh may seem to be suggesting that the rapist is, in some significant way, like the bird. Such a view would seem to be utterly lacking in morality! Yet the reference to cries and pain at the end of the poem lets us know that this at least is not a callous view. How, then, should we understand this view? What about right and wrong?

In his commentary on the poem, Nhat Hanh writes, "In my meditation I saw that if I had been born in the village of the pirate and raised in the same conditions as he was, I am now the pirate. I cannot condemn myself so easily." Clearly Nhat Hanh believes that our character is shaped to a significant degree by the conditions in which we are born and raised. Social science, of course, supports him in this, but Nhat Hanh's view here is largely based upon the Buddhist views of causation, interdependence, and *anātman* or no-self that we discussed above. Let us consider how they apply here.

Since there is no fixed human self, there is no fixed thing or essence in us that it would be appropriate to label "good" or "bad" in a static way, as if that defined the being of the person. Obviously the rapist has severely harmed the girl. Since causing pain is always wrong in Buddhism, we can certainly label this action of the pirate's "wrong," but we cannot take this one action as defining the being or innermost essence of the pirate—both because there is no such innermost essence and because there is more to the pirate than this one action. This way of thinking is what puts Buddhism in the position of seeing this deed as wrong without needing to condemn the pirate in toto.

Furthermore, as Nhat Hanh says, "all of us are to some extent responsible for this state of affairs." That is, again drawing upon the worldview that emphasizes causality and interdependence, we have all together constructed this world, in which the Western world is far richer than the developing world, in which people can be born into crushing poverty and hopelessness. We could make a difference in this state of affairs if we cared enough, made it a priority, and dedicated ourselves. The pirate is responsible for his actions (he could have chosen otherwise; not everyone who was born in his village and is as poor as he became a pirate); yet it is also the case that if the world were not as it is, he would not have become a pirate. It is quite reasonable for me to conclude, as Nhat Hanh says, that if I had been born and raised in the same conditions as the pirate, chances are very good that I would have turned out the same as he. There is no innermost essence or soul in me that differentiates me qualitatively from the pirate. Thus there is no place here for moral superiority; my impulse to look down upon the pirate as inferior to me is misplaced—he is largely the product of the conditions of his life, as am I. Consequently I cannot arrogate to myself a superior place, looking down from the distance of my moral

Vietnamese monk Thich Nhat Hanh has written of this, saying, "We were able to understand the suffering of both sides, the Communists and the anti-Communists. . . . That is why we did not take a side, even though the whole world took sides. . . . We wanted to stop the fighting, but the bombs were so loud. . . . We wanted reconciliation, we did not want a victory."

The above quotation also manifests a third element in Buddhist nonadversariality: universal compassion—caring about the suffering of others without limitation by nationality, ideology, race, or other dividing factor. Another example comes from Myanmar (Burma). Aung San Suu Kyi tells the story of a colleague in the democracy movement who was arrested and interrogated by the greatly feared military intelligence force: "When Uncle U Kyi Maung was under detention, one of the Military Intelligence officers interrogating him asked, 'Why did you decide to become a member of the National League for Democracy?' And he answered, 'For your sake.'" This kind of Buddhist compassion, which fundamentally recognizes no one as an enemy, bears considerable resemblance to the ideals of Christian love and may be easier for Westerners familiar with this tradition to understand than some other aspects of Buddhist ethics based in such concepts as karma or the nonexistence of a self.

Nonjudgmentalism is essential to Western Engaged Buddhist ethics as well. It is one of the primary lessons learned by Western Engaged Buddhists from their Asian teachers—the possibility, and even desirability, of engaging morally with concrete social issues without having to negatively judge the persons on the other side of these issues. Let us consider some examples.

The Buddhist Peace Fellowship is an American Engaged Buddhist network. Its journal, *Turning Wheel: The Journal of Socially Engaged Buddhism,* is one of the best places to find the work of American Engaged Buddhists. There are many examples in its pages of Americans (and occasionally other Western Buddhists) whose engagements with society demonstrate the virtue of Buddhist nonjudgmentalism. Jiko Linda Cutts, co-abbess of San Francisco Zen Center, reports on her experiences as part of a delegation (sponsored by the Fellowship of Reconciliation) visiting San Jose de Apartado, a peace community in

Colombia. She recounts that her delegation met with an army colonel who had been accused of human rights abuses, including torture.

My practice at this time was, "Can I hold to my intention not to abandon any being?" One of the practices of the delegation was just to listen. How could I stay open to this person, in spite of my judgments, and just listen? It was a very interesting and very difficult practice for me. . . . There was a group effort to be respectful, to listen, and to realize that this person is the way he is due to causes and conditions: his past, his upbringing, how he was indoctrinated, what happened to him. I reminded myself that with the same conditions, I might be in the same situation. I practiced not neglecting mindfulness while face to face with someone who thinks very differently from the way I think.

Clearly the writer is very much dedicated to the promotion of values of peace. Nevertheless, she intentionally makes an effort not to negatively judge someone who, at first appearance, seems to represent everything she opposes and actively works to eliminate.

We can also see in this passage how the author works through the ethical challenge before her as a form of Buddhist practice. We should begin by noting that she is not trying to suppress her immediate negative response to this person. Instead, she is following a kind of three-step process: she first needs to be aware of what her feelings actually are; then she brackets, or puts to the side, her personal thoughts and feelings while challenging herself to draw as near as possible to her ideal of nonjudgmentalism; finally, she tries to listen open-mindedly to what the man before her is saying. This three-step process is a form of Buddhist practice called "mindfulness"; it entails being fully aware of the present moment in the present moment. The practice is not to suppress one's own feelings but to be aware of them, then put them aside, and then give 100 percent of one's attention to the present moment—in this case, listening to a person speak. If one is able to follow this process, it opens the possibility that one may hear something that one had not anticipated and that one could not have heard if one was listening only partially to the other because one was partly thinking about one's own prejudgments. Sometimes one may

from both the Palestinian and Israeli sides—was the voice of victim-
hood, saying: "These crimes were committed against our people. We
will never forget. We cannot have peace until there is justice for these
crimes." This was the voice of righteous—that is, morally justified—
anger, the voice that feels it would be morally wrong, a further injury
to the injuries already suffered by our ancestors, if the people who
did this to our people were not made to suffer, if we were to let it go,
the voice that says: we will never forget. A Thai Buddhist laywoman,
Chatsumarn Kabilsingh (since ordained as Venerable Dhammananda
Bhikkhuni) finally said that she could not in her heart understand what
the Israelis and Palestinians were saying. She saw them as "nourishing
their suffering," whereas her training was "to let go of it." This remark
broke the ice among the Buddhists present, all of whom agreed that
this was how they were feeling.

Another insight into nonjudgmentalism came later on that same
trip, when the Peace Council visited Hebrew Union College on Holocaust Memorial Day and heard an intensely emotional presentation on
the Holocaust. Afterwards, Geshe Sopa, a Tibetan monk and distinguished scholar, spontaneously addressed the dean of the college. He
pointed out that Tibet had been invaded and occupied by the Chinese,
occasioning great suffering and loss of life in Tibet. When the Tibetans reflect upon this invasion and occupation, he said, they believe
that it happened because of their collective karma. They believe that
sometime in their past lives they, as a group, did something terrible
to the Chinese and that their present suffering is the result. He invited
the Israeli Jews to reflect on whether in a past life they may have been
German soldiers, doing bad things and earning bad karma as a result,
occasioning their present suffering. He concluded: The main thing is
to have compassion for mistakes made from an egocentric viewpoint,
from ignorance. Sometimes you have a wrong view that fills you with
hatred and you do something out of hatred that earns you negative
karma. That must be subject to our compassion, our love. The Chinese
are now earning terrible karma for what they are doing to us. We must
feel compassion for *all* who are suffering, on both sides. We don't look
at the Chinese as evil but try to find a peaceful solution and make them
happy and peaceful. Geshe Sopa spoke very similar words a few days

later to the director of the Deheishe Camp for Palestinian refugees. As might be expected, on both occasions his words were met by a stunned silence. This is in fact the starkest example I have ever witnessed of incommensurability: neither the Buddhists nor the Westerners present seemed to understand what the other was talking about.

Here we see the constellation of elements involved in Buddhist non-judgmentalism. There is compassion for everyone involved in the situation, based upon the understanding that people make terrible mistakes and do terrible things because we are egocentric and ignorant. There is nonadversariality in the belief that it is good for both the Chinese and the Tibetans for the Chinese to end their aggression against the Tibetans. There is the search for a win-win situation that will satisfy everyone. At the center of all this, there is rejection of the attachment to self (here in the form of the group self) that causes each side to skew its perspective in such a one-sided fashion that it can entirely overlook its own side's contribution to the problem, allowing each side to think that all the moral blame is on the other side while one's own side is entirely morally justified. There is of course utter rejection of the idea that one's own supposed moral righteousness and the other's supposed moral depravity can justify in any way either side's hatred and aggression toward the other.

The Buddhists present on this occasion particularly rejected the idea that justice, conceived as the vanquishing of the other side, was a prerequisite for the achievement of peace. To them such a way of thinking is a major impediment to peace. A nonjudgmental, Buddhist way of thinking about peace may be seen in the "People's Peace Plan" for Sri Lanka proffered by the Sarvodaya Shramadana as a way to the resolution of the conflict between that nation's Sinhalese and Tamil populations. Using the Buddhist Four Noble Truths as a template, the plan explicitly rejects the idea that the problem can be identified with either the Sri Lankan government or the Tamil Tigers and instead defines the problem as violence itself. It identifies the causes of the problem as poverty and ethnic conflict. The goal is a state of peace, defined as a sustainable, spiritually balanced island that works for all. Here one can see the avoidance of one-sided blaming (the problem is violence, not one side or the other); acknowledgement of the contri-

must begin by developing one's own inner peacefulness in order to be capable of bringing peace to society. In this way, spiritual practice, the attaining of traditional Buddhist spiritual goals, and the betterment of human life here and now blend into a seamless whole for the Engaged Buddhists.

Spirituality and Conceptual Teachings

Spirituality of course must fit harmoniously with conceptual teachings. In chapter 1, we saw that Buddhism has found room to embrace both the life of the village-dwelling monk, who engages with the layperson in society, and the eremitic life of the forest-, cave-, or mountain-dwelling monk, who intentionally separates himself from society in order to pursue intensive meditation in hopes of enlightenment. We are now ready to consider the possibility that the coexistence of the village bhikkhu and the forest- (cave-, mountain-) dwelling bhikkhu may suggest the presence of a conceptual tension within traditional Buddhism. Here we get at the spiritual heart of what is controversial about Engaged Buddhism.

Certainly one can look at traditional Buddhism and, in the light of that teaching, see many things that might lead a person to conclude that life as we know it—samsara—is intrinsically and irremediably flawed and that the wise will therefore cease caring about it, detach themselves from it, have as little as possible to do with it, and earnestly try to leave it. Consider, for example, the "Fire Sermon" of the Buddha, which reads in part as follows: "Bhikkhus, all is burning. And what, bhikkhus, is the all that is burning? The eye is burning, forms are burning . . . the ear is burning . . . the mind is burning. . . . Seeing thus, bhikkhus, the instructed noble disciple experiences revulsion towards the eye, towards forms . . . towards the ear . . . towards the mind. . . . Experiencing revulsion, he becomes dispassionate. Through dispassion [his mind] is liberated. . . . He understands: 'Destroyed is birth, the holy life has been lived, what had to be done has been done, there is no more for this state of being.'" It is not surprising that many Buddhists have taken teachings like this to mean that samsara is inherently flawed, that the correct response toward it is to feel revulsion and to flee it if at all possible.

Consider the charnel ground meditations (meditations on decaying bodies) and certain meditations on the body found in the *Foundations of Mindfulness Sutta*. (A *sutta* [Sanskrit, *sutra*] is a text that records the words of a Buddha.) Here the bhikkhus are instructed to contemplate the body in several contexts. They are invited to review the body as full of such so-called "impurities" as "feces, bile, phlegm, pus, blood, sweat, fat, tears, grease, spittle, snot, oil of the joints, and urine." They are also invited to contemplate the body as it decays on the charnel ground through several specified stages. The expected result of such contemplations is that the meditator will "not cling" to the body or to anything in the world. Thus there are times in tradition when one intentionally cultivates a sense of revulsion from the body, the world, and life as we know it in order to cultivate nonattachment toward them. This attitude of nonattachment and these sorts of practices seem to fit with a view of samsara as inherently unsatisfactory *(duḥkha)* and with the intention of practicing Buddhism in order to leave samsara once and for all. They seem to fit with the eremitic practices of the forest-, cave-, or mountain-dwelling bhikkhu or layman and even to an extent with monasticism itself, with its withdrawal from the family and normal societal life.

But there is more to Buddhism than this; the matter is more complex. Many texts express a more positive view of life in this world or give advice for living well in this world or advocate the cultivation of virtues that have nothing to do with leaving the world—virtues that in fact can be expressed only in the context of the relationships between human beings or between humans and other sentient beings. In other words, there are texts that give instructions for living in this world in a perfected manner. For example, there is the *Mettā Sutta*, the text that extols the virtue of *mettā*, or loving-kindness, which one should cultivate until one regards all beings in the same way that a mother regards her only child, ready to sacrifice her own life for the child's, out of her devotion to the child. There is the *Sigālovāda Sutta*, which gives concrete and sympathetic advice to the layperson, teaching how one should behave with respect to parents, spouses, children, friends, teachers, servants, and mendicants. There is the teaching given to kings that they should conform to the *dasarājadhamma*, the ten kingly

at it carefully, one can see that the problem is not the world as such but the human way of responding to the world. *Conceptually Engaged Buddhists embrace the second option—that is, they understand the goal of Buddhist practice as being liberation from* duḥkha *and the perfection of wisdom and compassion.* One does not hear Engaged Buddhists speaking of escaping from the wheel of samsara. However, this does not mean that they have given up the spiritual goals of Buddhism because they fully embrace the goal of eliminating *duḥkha* in *all* its senses, including worldly suffering from brutal governments, hunger, etc. *and* spiritual suffering from the human dis-ease of chronic dissatisfaction with life.

The Engaged Buddhist theoretician Buddhadasa Bhikkhu has argued articulately for this view: "Having not fully appreciated or examined the Buddha's teaching regarding *dukkha,* many people have misunderstood it. They have taken it to mean that birth, old age, sickness, death, and so on are themselves *dukkha.* In fact, those are just its characteristic vehicles. . . . Anything that clings or is clung to as 'I' or 'mine' is *dukkha.* Anything that has no clinging to 'I' or 'mine' is not *dukkha.* Therefore birth, old age, sickness, death, and so on, if they are not clung to as 'I' or 'mine,' cannot be *dukkha.*" This is a very important statement. Buddhadasa is saying that nonattachment, or not clinging, is the key to Buddhist spirituality. However, it is a mistake to think that what we have to be nonattached *to* is the world or the conditions of human life: being born, dying, etc. That is not the problem. The problem, he says, is the way we think about and relate to this human life. If I take this body and these thoughts to be myself, or "I," then I will naturally want this body and this thinking to persist. I will "cling" to them, insisting that they continue as "my" life, despite the fact that that is impossible because they must change and perish. In this way, I create *duḥkha.* This is perhaps the most fundamental form of *duḥkha:* my clinging to the constantly changing and mortal physical and mental events that constitute my existence, my labeling them as "I," my clinging to them as the most important things in the world, and my futile abhorrence and resistance of the inevitability of their demise. If we attempt to cure this problem by stopping the birth, old age, and dying (that is, by escaping from the wheel of samsara), we are focusing on the wrong thing. Birth and death are not the problem; clinging is the problem. That is what we need to focus on stopping. Thus nonattachment is not nonattachment to the world; it is the ending of clinging to the idea of "I" and the grasping that goes with it.

Buddhadasa's argument is by no means out of line with traditional Buddhism. All Buddhists agree that clinging to "I" is at the core of the problem of the human condition, the way in which we generate our own psycho-spiritual suffering, our *duḥkha*. If we can stop this clinging to the "I" and its cravings, we will become less selfish. Everyone also agrees that it is at the heart of Buddhist practice and goals not to be selfish. Clearly it is central to caring for others to get the "I, me, mine" out of the center of the picture. The engagement with the world that characterizes Engaged Buddhism is simply an expression of this caring. In this way, a very traditional Buddhist spirituality is insepa rable from the worldly engagement that defines Engaged Buddhism. This spirituality draws on one reading of the Buddhist scriptures (the one that says the problem is in our minds, not the world) rather than the other, but it does not invent that reading, which is as old as Buddhism itself.

Self and Other (I)

When we look at spiritual social activism, it is helpful to examine the relationship between self and other—in this case, the relationship between those who are the social activists and those who are the recipients of that activism. Often people rush into action without awareness of the importance of this relationship, but the wrong relationship between social activists and the communities they serve ("self" and "other") can poison social activism, no matter how good the intentions. Buddhism has a useful awareness of the intricacies of this relationship that is rooted in its classic teachings.

A good example of this can be found in the *Diamond Sutra*, one of the well-known scriptures from the Mahayana *prajñā-pāramitā*, or "perfection of wisdom" literature. These scriptures build on the earlier teachings of interdependence and no-self to teach *śūnyatā*, or emptiness. In brief, the idea of emptiness is that all things are utterly interdependent and mutually constructive, to the extent that (what might

in some cases adapted—to preparing a person for action in the world or for supporting such action. For example, any practice that helps to reduce self-centeredness will be very useful for Engaged Buddhist purposes, in addition to its usefulness for more traditional Buddhist spiritual purposes.

MEDITATION AND MINDFULNESS

Engaged Buddhists are interested in both the purely spiritual purposes of meditation and in its practical effects. In fact, the two cannot really be separated. A little reflection on the idea of inner peace demonstrates this point. One of the fruits of meditative concentration practice is inner peace. Inner peace is a spiritual goal in and of itself. In traditional Buddhism it has always been regarded as one of the marks of a person who is making spiritual progress. Engaged Buddhism introduces the additional spiritual challenge to maintain that inner peace at the very moment of engagement in active and difficult work in the world.

The signature contribution of Engaged Buddhism to spiritual social activism is the idea that work for world peace should be based upon a platform of inner peace. It happens that inner peace is very useful to the social activist. One aspect of inner peace is that it is a state of calm, relaxation, and composedness. Thus the inner peace generated in meditation is restorative for those working over long periods with intractable, frustrating, or dangerous conflict situations. In times of crisis, if one can maintain one's inner peace, one will be able to keep one's wits about one. For those who think that meditation is other-worldly, Thich Nhat Hanh points out that if everyone in a lifeboat is panicking, the situation is made even more dire. However, if even one person can maintain calm mindfulness, he may be able to do what needs to be done, calm others, and save many lives.

Insight meditation practices also turn out to be helpful in many ways for Engaged Buddhists. Insight meditation focuses on both inner and outer processes—for example, on listening to internally generated sounds such as one's own breathing and to external sounds such as the wind. Thus insight meditation is as likely to take one into the world as into one's own physical and mental processes. In either case, the practice develops one's mindfulness, or attention, to whatever one is focusing on. Thus those who practice mindfulness of an external phenomenon are developing the ability to perceive that phenomenon more intensely and fully, in all its rich particularity, moment by moment. In addition, they are training themselves to quiet the internal commentary and judgment that often accompanies perception, to let the perception, as far as possible, simply be. This is a traditional practice. If one adds one's caring, or the intention to be helpful, as Engaged Buddhists do, then one has a practice that can turn one's attention to the world with enhanced vividness, diminished internal commentary, and the will to respond to any suffering or problems that one may perceive. Such training should, if it works as promised, prepare one to be alert and ready to respond in an intelligent manner to the unpredictable situations that frequently come up in socially engaged work.

Even insight meditation practices that one might associate with ideas of escaping the world of samsara are often seen as helpful for Engaged Buddhists. For example, during the war years in Vietnam Thich Nhat Hanh strongly recommended the traditional graveyard meditations to his students. He urged them to meditate on the stages of decomposing corpses until they no longer felt either fear or revulsion but were calm and composed in the presence of death. They would thus be better prepared—not to flee samsara but to handle the death and carnage they might encounter in their work during the war and to face their own possible death in such dangerous work without fear. This would enable them better to evacuate a village caught between the opposing sides of a firefight or to hide a young man fleeing the army, at risk of their own lives.

LOVING-KINDNESS AND COMPASSION

Thich Nhat Hanh titles one of his books on Engaged Buddhism *Love in Action*, which is a good short definition of Engaged Buddhism. Buddhist ethics teach that intention is the root of action; not only does it constitute one's motivation, but it also constitutes the moral and karmic value of one's action. Love (or loving-kindness, *mettā*) and compassion are the mental states at the root of Engaged Buddhist action. It follows that an Engaged Buddhist, whose aspiration is to act for the welfare of others, should intentionally cultivate loving-kindness and

Glassman's most striking programs, "street retreats." Faced with home-lessness in New York City, Glassman developed a program to take stu-dents into the streets of the Bowery, where they live as the homeless do for several days—walking the streets all day without money, without a roof over their heads at night, panhandling, growing progressively dirtier by the day, and receiving looks of uneasiness/contempt/aver-sion from passersby. While Glassman acknowledges that his students' experience can never be the same as those of the truly homeless, it nonetheless is a profound experience generating insights and a quality of understanding unavailable by any other means. Many participants say it is the most profound experience of their lives. Programs develop out of such experience based, philosophically, upon seeing the other as not inherently different from oneself and, viscerally, upon freedom from feelings of uneasiness with the other.

It is perhaps human nature to feel some degree of uneasiness and discomfort with the unknown other, especially when that other looks unpleasant. Glassman's programs strive to eliminate the feeling of separation between oneself and the other at the foundation of that kind of uneasiness. They are grounded in a spiritual practice that he calls "bearing witness"—being together with the other, in relationship with the other, in a state of nonjudgmental open-mindedness. By not separating oneself from the other—that is, by taking active steps to overcome the initial feeling of separation—one enters into a condi-tion of not-knowing, in which one's ideas about what it's like to be the other—in this case, to live on the streets—and the judgments that go with those ideas are repeatedly shattered.

For Glassman, not-knowing is the source of all knowledge. Here Glassman's spirituality falls right in line with traditional Zen spiritual-ity. Traditional Zen master Shunryu Suzuki titled his modern classic on Zen spirituality *Zen Mind, Beginner's Mind*, stating that the expert's mind is too full to learn anything while the beginner's mind is wide open. It is the beginner's mind that is needed in Zen—the challenge is to maintain that beginner's mind! Glassman is so much in harmony with this spirituality that not-knowing is one of the three basic tenets of the Zen Peacemaker Order that he founded—namely, (1) not-knowing, giving up fixed ideas about ourselves and the universe; (2)

bearing witness to the joy and suffering of the world; and (3) loving actions toward ourselves and others. Here "not-knowing" is to cultivate an open mind, a practice strongly supported by "bearing witness." "Loving actions toward ourselves and others" is the central practice of both traditional Buddhism and Engaged Buddhism. For Glassman it is given direction by not-knowing and bearing witness.

Self and Other (II)

As spiritual disciplines, being with others and working with others have the ability to bring about significant changes in the relationship between self and other. This is one reason they are such important practices in some Engaged Buddhist groups. Two useful examples of how they work are the projects of Bernie Glassman and the Tzu Chi movement. They will make clear that social action and spiritual development are two sides of a single coin.

Regarding his work in helping inner-city homeless Americans, Glassman writes, "My own interest in feeding others—in what people call social action—has a lot to do with what I can learn from the people I seem to be helping. By becoming one with them, by seeing the world as much as I can through their eyes, I learn what their needs are. At the same time, I broaden and expand my own view of life." Here we don't see the full-blown eradication of all sense of "self" and "other" to which the *Diamond Sutra* refers, but we do see a kind of practical living-out of the ideal. Glassman immediately restates the ideal of "becoming one with [the homeless]" as "seeing the world as much as I can through their eyes." This is perhaps a more attainable goal and one that he means very literally and works for in the street retreats. Everyone concerned benefits from Glassman and the other activists trying to do this. It benefits the homeless to have their true needs met; Glassman emphasizes that this goal can be achieved only through a process in which the activists are able to put aside their own thoughts and beliefs regarding what the homeless need and try as far as possible to hear what the homeless are saying in the way that they themselves intend it, to see as the homeless are seeing.

For two reasons it is also important for the spiritual development of the activists, Glassman's students, that they be *able* to put down their

preconceptions, that they be *able* to truly hear what the other is saying as it is intended. First, it is a part of classic Buddhist mindfulness
training to be present in the moment without preconceptions, judgment, or commentary. In working to be "one with [the homeless],"
Glassman's students spend time with the homeless, trying as far as
possible to put aside their preconceptions, make no judgments, and
engage in no mental commentary, to be fully engaged in and by the
present moment of being-in-this-place-now-with-these-people, without the kind of thoughts that separate them from the present moment
of experience (thoughts that, figuratively, stand at a distance, making
their observations and commentaries). Of course one can always question to what extent it is possible to fully put down one's own perspective and take up another's. It is very easy to think that one is doing so
and still project one's own perspective upon the other. Such questions,
however, are all grist for the mill in the Zen practice of questioning
everything or Glassman's practice of unknowing. Students are encouraged to ask those questions, too, and follow where they lead.

Second, as Glassman says, the homeless have their own experience
and understanding; these have their own validity, which the students
(and anyone) would be broadened by learning. Not that one necessar-
ily adopts that (or any) particular point of view, but it is a certain experience of truth and reality, and it is helpful to spend some time with it.
Let us look at this more closely. In Buddhist understanding, every perspective on life is a partial experiential realization of truth. One is not
interested here in putting together as many such perspectives as one
can in the hopes that added up, they will somehow bring one closer to
a full perception of truth. Rather, by getting inside a number of perspectives, one recognizes the partiality of each such perspective, very
much including one's own. That recognition helps one to hold one's
own perspective more loosely, and this, in turn, is an important step in
moving toward a fuller perception of truth. Moreover, each perspective, while representing only a partial apprehension of lived truth, is
nonetheless a partial apprehension, valid as such. One can gain a certain amount of insight if one can get inside it, even for a time. One does
learn from it. So Glassman is sincere in his belief that his students have
as much to gain from working with the poor as the poor have to gain

from Glassman's students. The gains may be of different kinds, but it would be difficult to say which are more important. Certainly Glassman's students stand to gain in their development of traditional, core Buddhist spiritual values such as selflessness, mindfulness, and insight. As we have discussed, Engaged Buddhism does *not* mean putting aside traditional Buddhist spirituality. It means cultivating and expressing such spirituality at least partially through social engagement.

The work of the Tzu Chi movement is based upon a similar insight into the relationship between the giver and the recipient. Like Glassman, Venerable Cheng Yen understands her disciples' working with this relationship as key to their achieving traditional Buddhist spiritual goals. Her movement is based on the giving of medical, material, and loving care to the sick, the poor, the elderly, and the victims of natural disasters. But this is only half of the giving in this movement. As Cheng Yen puts it, "The poor and wretched receive help, the rich and fortunate activate their love, and thus both can be grateful to each other." It is equally important for her followers to have the opportunity to "activate their love" as for the needy to receive help. This movement is for the benefit of both the needy and the fortunate. In fact, the fortunate are not so entirely fortunate. Cheng Yen speaks of the empty lives that many of her followers had before they became active members of Tzu Chi. Living comfortable lives, many were still lonely and depressed or felt their lives were meaningless. They call to mind Siddhartha Gautama in the palace, uneasily dissatisfied with his life of luxury. It seems that humankind needs something more. But it is not always easy to find that something more. In Cheng Yen's program the needy are seen as giving the fortunate something real and needed—the opportunity to develop their compassion, thereby developing their spirituality and inner peace and joy.

Cheng Yen advises her followers, "Give whatever you can, whether a little or a lot. Strive persistently with equanimity and patience. You will soon reach the level at which 'There is no giver, there is no receiver, there is no gift.' Giving and receiving will be nothing more than part of the natural order of things." Here, then, is the fully developed spirituality of the *Diamond Sutra*. It is a fact that the needy give the fortunate something precious in giving them the opportunity to develop their

up some of its implications (and many similar ideas in the Buddha's teachings) and found in them two closely related ideas that are important for the way Buddhism functions in the modern world of religious pluralism, in which different religions constantly interact. First, it is a short step to conclude that if Buddhism is a means to an end, probably all religions should be seen as means to an end, as tools for developing spiritual values. Buddhists who think this way seem to put aside the question of whether the ends of these different paths are exactly the same and simply look at the many religions as means or tools for spiritual practice. Many Engaged Buddhists clearly feel that the basic values expressed in the major religions—values such as love, wisdom, and selflessness—are the same. Buddhism possesses these values, but the evidence shows that it does not possess them *exclusively*. This being the case, there is nothing to preclude the Engaged Buddhists from expressing their esteem of other religions as other tools for developing love, wisdom, and selflessness and encouraging people who follow those other paths to follow them devotedly. This is one strong source of the inter-religious friendliness that we see in Engaged Buddhism. The Dalai Lama has said that if someone has practiced Buddhism seriously for years and has failed to clearly benefit from it, then that person should consider practicing another religion. Buddhism is pragmatic; it looks for results—specifically the elimination of *duḥkha*. Religions are tools to that end. Clearly Buddhists, Engaged and otherwise, feel that Buddhism is an effective and perhaps superior tool, but other religions are tools as well. They should all be evaluated by their effectiveness; this, in turn, is best gauged by observing its long-term practitioners.

Second, perhaps one can and should distinguish between the Buddhist religion and the Dharma. "Dharma" is a very broad term, untranslatable into English and includes meanings of truth, reality, and the teachings of the Buddha—teachings that Buddhists believe express truth and disclose reality. The Buddha teaches the Dharma, but is the Dharma identical to the Buddhist religion? Many Engaged Buddhists believe that at least a great part of the Dharma is an expression of a universal spirituality. This is an expression of their confidence in the truth of the Dharma, but by the same token it is an expression of their (in a sense) nonownership of it. Some Engaged Buddhists—

notably the Dalai Lama and Thich Nhat Hanh—are extremely skilled at expressing their teachings in the language of a kind of universal spirituality rather than a specifically Buddhist terminology. The language of this universal spirituality is the same as the basic values that they see expressed in other religions as well. Buddhadasa, for instance, believes that all religions teach selflessness and offer practices that help us to become less self-centered. The Dalai Lama often says, "My religion is kindness," and he urges people to practice "universal responsibility." Behind these words are the specifically Buddhist ideas of *anātman* (no-self), *karuṇā* (compassion), *mettā* (loving-kindness), and the vows of the bodhisattva, but there is no need to use these particular words, especially since words, in Buddhism, are very imperfect means of expressing a truth that is experiential, not verbal, in nature.

The Engaged Buddhists, with their commitments to this spirituality, its truth and effectiveness, are in a good position to differentiate between this spirituality—that is, the Dharma—and the Buddhist religious institutions (including verbal teachings) that, hopefully, carry, teach, and manifest the Dharma. Once this differentiation is made, it is clear that their primary loyalty is to the Dharma, whereas they may find that Buddhist religious institutions, depending on the case, are functioning well or need some reform, criticism, or development.

Sulak Sivaraksa, a Thai lay Engaged Buddhist leader, is a good example of this. He differentiates between what he calls "Big B Buddhism" and "little b buddhism." Little b buddhism is what we referred to above as the Dharma; Sulak particularly emphasizes the importance of selflessness, awareness, and loving-kindness as expressed in one's behavior. To him it is irrelevant whether one formally becomes a Buddhist. Sulak has subjected Big B Buddhism, especially as it exists in his home country, to scathing criticism. He sees mainstream Big B Thai Buddhism as fossilized, overemphasizing meaningless rituals; delivering the teachings in a stultifying form that does not convey the profound challenge of the Dharma to modern humanity; and—because of its symbiotic relationship with the Thai government—guilty of Thai nationalism, chauvinism, and militarism, values antithetical to the Dharma. In classic reformist manner, he uses the Dharma to criticize institutionalized Buddhism and push for its reform.

Thich Nhat Hanh, in a different situation, took a different approach. Knowing that the Vietnam War had been partly caused by the struggle for ideological supremacy between the United States and the Soviet Union during the Cold War, he was acutely aware of the direct harm that adherence to ideology could cause. Consequently he did not want Buddhism to act like another ideology, capable of dividing people and causing antagonism among divided groups. His teaching has always stressed the importance of remembering that the *forms* in which the Dharma can be expressed must be flexible since they are not the essential part (the Dharma is). The very first precept of his Tiep Hien order states, "Do not be idolatrous about or bound to any doctrine, theory, or ideology, even Buddhist ones. All systems of thought are guiding means; they are not absolute truth." This precept echoes the Parable of the Raft and demonstrates how the latter opens the door to considerable flexibility about the form in which the "guiding means" are expressed. Thich Nhat Hanh cites the saying that the Buddha taught "10,000 Dharma doors" and invites others to open even more. Certainly he has opened quite a few himself! Here is one of the sources of the tremendous creativity of the Engaged Buddhists.

There is at least one additional reason for the inter-religious friendliness of Engaged Buddhism that must be acknowledged: loving-kindness, or what Tzu Chi calls in English "unconditional love." In 2003 Tzu Chi began a relationship with an Islamic boarding school in Indonesia. This school began after Muslim mobs in Jakarta rioted against the ethnic Chinese community. The founder of the school, a Muslim, wanted to teach Islam in a spirit of compassion and love, free of intolerance. Over time the school had so many students—mostly orphans and students from poor families—that it could not feed them all. The students needed food, so Tzu Chi gave them food, out of the unconditional love that they have for all people. They declared that unconditional love is unconditional; it cannot be stopped by differences, religious or any other kind. The relationship begun in this way has grown. The staff and students of the school all became Tzu Chi volunteers. Tzu Chi promised to help build a new school building, and its volunteers attended a celebration of the Prophet Mohammed's birthday, in a spirit of friendliness toward the Muslim faith. The result, as far as Tzu Chi is concerned, is mutual love growing between the Muslim and Chinese communities.

These events are one example of a final point regarding the inter-religious friendliness of Engaged Buddhism: it is an essential part of its peacemaking. This ecumenical spirit is based upon the deeper values we have discussed above and is not a means to an end; however, Engaged Buddhism could not achieve its peacemaking goals without it. If peace is finally based in goodwill among communities, then inter-communal, inter-cultural, and inter-religious relations are an integral part of the work, and Tzu Chi was taking a direct step toward it in working with the Islamic school. Thich Nhat Hanh often says that love (or goodwill) and understanding are two sides of the same coin. He gives the example of a girl who snaps angrily at her brother when he goes to wake her. He feels angry until he remembers that she coughed a lot during the night and must be sick. When he remembers that, he understands, and his anger dissipates. This is a very simple example, but on a larger scale, the Engaged Buddhists believe that understanding among communities is a necessary foundation of good relations. Since religion is extremely important to most people, respectful understanding toward another community's religion is a necessary part of this foundation.

In this way, to some Engaged Buddhists building or expressing inter-religious friendliness is an integral part of the praxis of peacemaking. I will mention two more examples. During the Struggle Movement in Vietnam (the Buddhist movement to end the war), there were tensions between the Catholic minority and the Buddhist majority because of the suppression of Buddhism by the Catholic ruler, Ngo Dinh Diem. A young laywoman, Nhat Chi Mai, part of Thich Nhat Hanh's group, immolated herself as a self-sacrifice to awaken people and help bring peace to Vietnam. When she prepared to offer her life, she placed before herself statues of the Virgin Mary and the Buddhist Bodhisattva of Compassion, Kuan Yin. She knelt before these two statues in a position of worship as she gave her life, embodying in her very posture the reconciliation of the two communities; this reconciliation was a necessary component of the peace that she hoped to bring into being with her sacrifice.

One last point regarding Engaged Buddhism's ecumenical spirit may be added: Engaged Buddhism embodies an answer to a particular postmodern dilemma that may be stated as follows: In the postmodern world, as we become more familiar with a number of religions, the exclusivist view that only one religion (always "my" religion, whatever it is) is true and possesses saving or liberating power comes to seem both more and more unlikely and more and more reprehensible. The role of religion in causing or abetting violent conflict and war seems reason enough to many to try to overcome religious enmity, but in addition, greater familiarity with a number of religions has caused many people to see such enmity as foolish since many of the *ethical* teachings of the major religions, if not their theological and metaphysical teachings, seem to be compatible and mutually supportive. Many people find a certain amount of truth, a certain amount of inspiration, and certainly admirable saintly behavior in several religions. This draws them toward some degree of inter-religious friendliness. On the other hand, there *are* differences among religions, especially theological and metaphysical differences, and most people agree that if one is going to seriously practice a religion, one needs a certain amount of focus and dedication over time; spreading oneself too thin among many religions seems like an unproductive approach. What, then, should one do?

The inter-religious friendliness and ecumenical spirit that we have seen among the Engaged Buddhists is one response to this challenge. Largely because of the distinction between the Dharma and the Buddhist religion, the Engaged Buddhists have no problem being fully committed to Buddhism while sincerely seeing a great deal to commend and work together with in other religions. The only requirement is that those other religions manifest the Dharma—that is, selflessness, loving-kindness, and compassion—in their own idiom. In this way, Engaged Buddhist teachings have a particular, Buddhist, form that enables Engaged Buddhists to draw upon the strengths of a tradition that has been developing its practices for two and a half millennia, but they can recognize and embrace their common ground with others. We may note that the Dalai Lama himself is a great example of such a postmodern spirituality. He is simultaneously the head of the Tibetan Buddhist spiritual community, the very embodiment of Buddhism itself in the minds of millions, and a great cross-cultural religious leader who speaks a universalist spiritual language that goes right to the heart of millions of non-Buddhists.

In our era many people believe that there are two religious options. One must choose, they believe, between (1) conservative religion, sometimes manifesting as fundamentalism, which preserves traditional beliefs and strict morality from the degrading influences of modernity and liberalism and which is invariably exclusivist in outlook, believing it holds the only truth; and (2) a secularized world with liberal religion that is able to be friendly toward other religions. More conservative people are often offended by the latter, believing that it is a morally lax and spineless choice that allows us to give in when too much is demanded of us in either belief or behavior and to give up ground to other religions for mere worldly reasons (that is, the desire for peace); to conservatives, this is religion that gives in to science, gives in to academia, and gives in to other religions.

Those who believe that these are the only two possibilities are wrong; there is a third option. Engaged Buddhism is a religious path that is liberal yet demanding and challenging. It makes great demands upon the individual, who is challenged to measure up to ever higher spiritual standards of insight, wisdom, personal morality, loving-kindness, and compassion, as well as socially engaged standards of putting one's insights and values into practice energetically, selflessly, and courageously. It is intense and demanding, but not by embracing an understanding of morality as a matter of obedience to the external demands of a divine law, an approach that often characterizes more conservative religions. Rather, Engaged Buddhism is demanding in a way that comes from within—it understands itself to be holding up a very lofty ideal to which, because we are all endowed with *chanda,* or the wholesome urge to self-betterment and goodness, we are naturally attracted. Or, to use a Mahayana way of speaking, the Engaged Buddhist ideal is an expression of the Buddha nature within each person. The Buddha nature inherently responds to this ideal, which is just an expression of itself. In either formulation, the ideal pulls at us from

against the Chinese in his defense, the Dalai Lama fled Tibet and took up residence in Dharamsala, India, on land offered by the government of India. He continues to live there to this day with an expatriate Tibetan community. In working with his situation vis-à-vis the Chinese, the Dalai Lama has held consistently to the following principles: nonviolence; nonenmity; compassion for all; the importance of human rights; and the goal of reconciliation.

The Dalai Lama is one of the advocates of uncompromising nonviolence among the Engaged Buddhists. Of course according to the faithful, he is the incarnation of Avalokitesvara, the Bodhisattva of Compassion, and in fact his advocacy of nonviolence has a great deal to do with his adherence to what could be called principled compassion. The bottom line is that the Dalai Lama does not want to cause harm to any living being. And yet, of course, it is not acceptable that China has annexed Tibet; a positive response that will be in the interests of all must be found. A professed admirer of Gandhi, the Dalai Lama, like Gandhi, looks for assertive and constructive methods of advancing the welfare of all without harming any.

In many respects, the position of the Dalai Lama is prefigured in the *Dhammapada,* the ancient scriptural text from which many of the Engaged Buddhists draw heavily. It states, "All (mental) states have mind as their forerunner, mind is their chief, and they are mind-made. If one speaks or acts with a defiled mind, then suffering follows one even as the wheel follows the hoof of the draught-ox. All (mental) states have mind as their forerunner, mind is their chief, and they are mind-made. If one speaks or acts with a pure mind, happiness follows one as one's shadow that does not leave one. . . . Whatever harm a foe may do to a foe, or a hater to another hater, a wrongly-directed mind may do one harm far exceeding these."

This passage is based upon traditional Buddhist ideas of karma and no-self. As beings without a fixed self or soul, we construct "ourselves" and the events that make up "our" lives moment by moment by the choices we make. In those choices, the most important determining factor is the mental attitude or intention behind an action, inasmuch as it is the attitude or intention that determines the nature of the karmic seed that we plant with our action, whether that action be a thought, word, or deed. This is what the above passage means when it says that all mental states are mind-made. We therefore need to be very attentive to our mental states in order to avoid causing ourselves harm. If we indulge negative attitudes and mental states such as hatred, anger, or desire for vengeance, we will end up harming ourselves because these negative mental states will cause us to act in a way that will earn us negative karma; for example, our anger and desire for revenge will cause us to lash out violently at another, and this lashing out will earn us a painful karmic consequence in this or a future lifetime. We need to be particularly vigilant about our mental states when we are in a stressful or dangerous situation in which negative mental states would be likely.

When the text states that another person cannot do one as much harm as one can do to oneself, it means that while another can harm me physically or even kill me, that is the limit of what he can do. He actually harms *himself* karmically by acting violently. If a person dies, in this Buddhist worldview, he will have another life—in fact many more lifetimes—so death is not as great a harm as the person could cause himself by an angry state of mind because if he dies without a negative mental state, the future life will be a good one, whereas if he allows himself angry thoughts, words, and deeds, he will earn a painful future life. Clearly a belief in rebirth is crucial to this worldview. The Tibetans have this belief. Looking at things as they do, it is wiser and in their own interest to pursue a nonviolent course in the struggle for Tibetan autonomy; they would be harming themselves karmically if they fought the Chinese in a violent fashion. (This thinking is reinforced by the fact that Chinese military might overshadows Tibetan strength like an elephant outweighs a gnat.) Moreover, this kind of thinking is why the Tibetan leadership often speaks sorrowfully of the harm that the Chinese are doing *themselves* by causing so much harm to the Tibetan people, the biosphere, and culture; they are looking at the situation from the perspective of karma.

Another *Dhammapada* passage reads as follows: "Hatred is never appeased by hatred in this world; it is appeased by nonhatred. This is an eternal Law." This passage is extremely important among the Engaged Buddhists. Again, it is based upon karmic thinking. Karma

which to focus. In order for human society to survive and flourish, we must nurture and enhance our innate capacity for compassion, which is rooted in our ability to empathize, and work together as a society to weaken those societal and institutional structures and forces that strengthen our tendencies toward cruelty and violence.

All of this makes a good deal of sense and in many respects is unarguable. However, the Dalai Lama goes beyond this emphasis on empathy, compassion, and goodwill to rethink the concept of the "enemy." He often remarks that all humans are the same inasmuch as we all want happiness. Everything we do is done in an effort to be happy. We may seek happiness, however, in a way distorted by ignorance—ignorance based upon our lack of knowledge of others and their circumstances, our misinterpretations of our own experience, or misinformation we have been taught—or our excessive grasping owing to fear or egotism. It helps us to tone down our negative feelings toward our enemies when we remember that they, like we, are seeking happiness, in however distorted a way. It also may show us a way to proceed—trying to give our enemies more knowledge of us or to reduce their fear of us, for example.

Ultimately the Dalai Lama takes a step in his rethinking of the enemy that seems entirely counterintuitive to most people: he regards the enemy as a friend. This perspective is unique and one of his most challenging teachings. He writes, "Our enemy is very useful to us because, in order to practice compassion we need to practice tolerance, forgiveness, and patience, [and thus] we need someone to create some trouble. From this point of view, there is no need to feel anger toward the enemy. . . . In fact, we should feel gratitude for the opportunity he provides us." In order to make sense of such a teaching, we must recall the Buddhist view of human life: the present life is only one of a countless series of lives that we live, and the purpose of this entire vast stretch of experience is to progress spiritually. Considered in this context, the idea that the enemy helps us is perfectly rational. Outside of that spiritual context, perhaps we can think of this teaching in the same way that we think of a Zen koan or a parable of Jesus: it is so counterintuitive that it may startle us profoundly, opening up the possibility of a leap to an entirely new level of understanding or insight. It certainly may startle one into becoming aware of the way in which one is responding to an enemy, thus opening the door to greater self-knowledge on that point and possibly a more self-disciplined and constructive response.

Often people say that while nonviolence is a great ideal, one has to be realistic about it; a person should be nonviolent insofar as he should not attack others, but if he is attacked, he certainly must be free to use violence in his own defense, especially if he has tried other means, such as diplomacy and pressure tactics, and all other means have failed. It is striking in the Tibetan case that the leadership refuses to avail itself of this last-ditch fallback plan of using violence, even though the Tibetans have faced the worst-case scenario of foreign invasion and annexation.

The Tibetan leadership's main response to the Chinese invasion and annexation of Tibet has been a series of peace proposals and calls for talks. The Five-Point Peace Plan, which is the best known of these, calls for the following:

1. Transformation of the whole of Tibet into a zone of peace.
2. Abandonment of China's population-transfer policy, which threatens the very existence of the Tibetans as a people.
3. Respect for the Tibetan people's fundamental human rights and democratic freedoms.
4. Restoration and protection of Tibet's natural environment and the abandonment of China's use of Tibet for the production of nuclear weapons and dumping of nuclear wastes.
5. Commencement of earnest negotiations on the future of Tibet and of relations between the Tibetan and Chinese peoples.

Notice the importance of nonviolence in this plan. In addition to the protection of the lives and well-being of the Tibetan people (included in their fundamental human rights in point 3, a subject to be further discussed in chapter 6), point 4 calls for the restoration and protection of Tibet's natural environment. This is a part of nonviolence and peacemaking about which the Tibetans care a great deal. The occupation of Tibet by the Chinese has resulted in not only a huge amount of human death and suffering, but violence to many Tibetan plants and animals and to the Tibetan ecosphere as well. Chinese policies of agriculture, hunting, mining, and logging, combined with the fragility of Tibet's high-altitude ecosphere, have caused the extinction or near extinction of many species through habitat destruction and the decimation of entire herds with automatic weapons; deforestation of almost half the previously standing forests of Tibet, largely by clear-cutting; desertification of grasslands and slopes; serious water siltation and contamination, a particularly grave problem given that Tibet is Asia's principal watershed, with nearly half the world's population dependent upon rivers originating in Tibet; and deadly chemical and radioactive pollution of earth, water, and soil.

Matters regarding the environment and biota are very high on the Tibetans' list of concerns, as is evidenced not only by their prominence in point 4, but also by their inclusion in point 1, the transformation of Tibet into a zone of peace. The zone of peace is an important concept in the Tibetans' overall vision not only of making peace with China, but also of serving humanity by fulfilling Tibet's potential as a land and people. As a zone of peace, the entirety of Tibet would become the world's largest natural park, with humanity and nature living in harmonious balance, with laws protecting plant and animal life, and with the use of natural resources regulated to prevent damage to the ecosystem, including the prohibition of manufacturing that causes the production of hazardous wastes, such as nuclear wastes. In addition, the zone of peace idea is a response to issues of military power—all armaments would be strictly prohibited and the entirety of the country demilitarized—and geopolitical balance—Tibet would serve as a demilitarized neutral zone separating the great powers of India and China. The concept is pro-active on peacemaking, with a priority given to directing national resources and policies toward the active promotion of peace and environmental protection. Finally, the idea draws on Tibet's spiritual strengths and expresses the hope that Tibet could become a place where people from all over the world could come to find and develop inner peace. Thus the concept of a zone of peace suggests that there are many different dimensions involved in living in peace. Freedom from all military concerns is only the beginning. In addition, harmony between humanity and the natural world, contributing one's unique potential for the good of the world, and the development of personal inner peace are all part of making and sustaining peace.

Such are the ideas and principles promoted by the Tibetan leadership in its effort to gain autonomy from the Chinese. It must be reported that as of this writing no visible progress has been made in realizing this goal. The Tibetan leadership had depended upon the support of the international community in its struggle, but the international community has been very reluctant to press the Chinese on this issue. There is one small glimmer of hope, however. The Chinese Communist revolution intentionally attacked traditional culture within China and forcibly destroyed many Chinese people's traditional religious beliefs and values. The Communist leadership attempted to replace traditional religion in people's hearts with Communist ideology as an ideal to look up to and as a guiding ideology. Since the end of the Cultural Revolution, however, Communist ideology has fallen to a very low level as an ideal, and something of a spiritual vacuum has developed in many people's lives. In this context, Tibet has taken on an ironic new appeal to many Chinese. The Tibetan leadership's decision to maintain the ethical upper ground with its stance of principled pacifism, together with other obvious demonstrations of spirituality—such as the Dalai Lama's steadfast goodwill to all (importantly including the Chinese) and his cheerfulness in the face of adversity—have contributed to Tibet's coming to be seen by many among the younger generations of Chinese as a kind of Shangri-la, a place of great spirituality. For them an idealized Tibet offers a spirituality and a set of ideals that nothing in increasingly materialistic China can match. As the older generation of Chinese leaders dies off, if this view of Tibet remains popular among the younger generation, perhaps it will be sufficient for them to prevail upon a new generation of Chinese leaders at least to pursue policies in Tibet that are friendlier to the maintenance of traditional Tibetan religion. It is a faint hope, but it is an outcome that would not surprise the Tibetan leadership. The Dalai Lama often says that if there is inherent truth and value in Buddhism, it cannot help but survive; truth is more powerful than anything and eventually always prevails. He also takes a very long-term view, difficult for most Westerners to understand. Think of it this way: at the time that

of government pro-war and repressive policies. There were many acts of noncooperation with the government, including strikes, mass resignations from government positions, boycotts, return of government licenses, and the refusal to serve in the military; these moves were met by brutal reprisals. An underground network was formed to hide and protect military deserters and draft resisters and sometimes help them escape the country. Frequent massive street demonstrations, led by Buddhist monks and students, demanded the freedom to practice Buddhism (when the government was Catholic) and for an end to the war or called for free elections. Members of the movement worked closely with sympathetic governments, conferring regularly with top levels of such governments on policy issues. At the end, when the military crackdown on the movement was under way, many households placed their sacred family altars in the streets in the path of approaching tanks—a final, desperate plea to the soldiers to remember their deeper values and respect the people's desire for peace.

A word must be said on the self-immolations of Vietnamese Buddhist monks, nuns, and laypeople that occurred during the war years. In 1963 at a crossroads in downtown Saigon, the venerable monk Thich Quang Duc sat in the lotus posture, entered into deep meditative control, and burned himself to death without a sound or movement; he did so in protest of the Saigon regime's repression of Buddhism. His action revived an ancient practice of self-immolation that had existed in East Asia centuries previously and opened the door to the many further self-immolations by Vietnamese monks, nuns, and laypeople that ensued. These actions were broadcast on television into American living rooms, stunning the American public, who had difficulty understanding why someone would do such a shocking thing and how anyone could sit silent and immobile while his or her body burned. What did it all mean?

There is a tradition of self-immolation in Vietnam that traces back to the *Lotus Sutra*. The ancient intentions behind self-immolation included making an offering to the Buddha, imitating the bodhisattvas, and protesting oppression of the Dharma. In 1963 the Catholic Diem regime of South Vietnam was seriously repressing Buddhism, despite the fact that Vietnam was 80 percent Buddhist. When Thich Quang

Duc immolated himself, he did so with the traditional motivation of protesting oppression of the Dharma. This action, though it had not occurred in centuries, was culturally and religiously well understood in Vietnam; a bodhisattva would be expected to protect the Dharma. Gradually subsequent self-immolations turned more and more to the effort to stop the war; this also made sense to the Vietnamese, as a bodhisattva would also be expected to protect the people. Thich Nhat Hanh has explained that the self-immolations were an effort to communicate the suffering of war. They were an effort to reach the hearts of those who were prosecuting the war and to touch something there that would make them unwilling to continue to prosecute the war. The self-immolators were taking the action of nonhatred discussed in the *Dhammapada*—in this case a dramatic and powerful action able to sow powerful seeds of change. They were bodhisattvas acting out of love, sacrificing themselves in order to protect the lives of others.

While these actions are highly admired, even venerated, among most Mahayana Buddhists, they are not entirely without controversy in the Buddhist world. To take one's own life is clearly prohibited in the Vinaya, the book of rules governing the lives of Buddhist monastics. It is understood to violate the first lay precept against the taking of life. On the other hand, a Mahayana text, the *Skill in Means Sutra*, allows a bodhisattva to take life in order to save lives as long as the intention is pure and altruistic. The text admits that taking a life violates Buddhist ethics, meriting negative karma, but goes on to say that since the bodhisattva willingly accepts this negative karma for the sake of helping others, this self-sacrificing motivation outweighs the negativity of the act of taking a life, and the karma earned, in the end, is positive. Since Theravada Buddhists do not accept this text, they have a variety of views about this issue. Some of them think that Mahayana Buddhists are wrong in regarding self-immolation as morally good; others think that it is all right for Mahayana Buddhists to do it but that it would be wrong for a Theravada Buddhist. Maha Ghosananda referred to it as *dāna-pāramitā*, the perfection of giving. Most Mahayana Buddhists regard the self-immolators as bodhisattvas and venerate their actions as superhuman deeds of love, compassion, and veneration of the Dharma.

In addition to the actions taken in order to end the war, the Struggle Movement also took many actions for the protection, relief, and healing of the Vietnamese and for the reconstruction of their lives. Perhaps the best known of these was the Buddhist role in evacuating villages about to be caught in the crossfire of a battle. Buddhist monks and nuns, dressed in their bright yellow robes and carrying Buddhist flags for visibility, entered into the villages and walked the villagers out, while armies waited on both sides to engage the battle. At other times monastics helped establish cease-fire lines outside of villages by approaching both sides at considerable personal risk and convincing them to retreat to lines at a distance from the village. Buddhist social workers rebuilt destroyed villages, sometime rebuilding the same village repeatedly. They provided medical care and psychological counseling. They worked on behalf of war orphans, sometimes bringing them to family-like orphanages that they themselves had built and staffed with "grandparents," elderly people who had lost their own families in the war. At other times they provided money so that the orphans' relatives could afford to take them in and feed them. They continued their programs of rural development, teaching agricultural methods, sanitation, simple medicine, and so forth.

The actions of the Struggle Movement were very effective. The movement successfully gave voice and direction to the majority's desire for the war to end, leaving no doubt about the wishes of the people and putting pressure on successive governments to heed those wishes. It succeeded in bringing down a number of South Vietnamese governments that, in the people's view, were too interested in prosecuting or expanding the war and replacing them with governments more interested in pursuing negotiations with the North. In 1966, just before it was crushed, the Struggle Movement seemed on the verge of winning the struggle; it had the support of most sectors of the country, including the civil service, the police, and major divisions of the army, both generals and troops, who refused direct orders to crack down on the movement. Finally, the troops who had declared for the Struggle Movement were lured away, and troops loyal to the Saigon government, using American arms, tanks, and bases, cracked down on the movement, leaving the Buddhist pagodas that served as headquarters of the movement looking like charnel houses. Though the movement did not succeed politically, Thich Nhat Hanh has pointed out that it was not altogether a failure either. "The success of a nonviolent struggle can be measured only in terms of the love and nonviolence attained, not whether a political victory was achieved. In our struggle in Vietnam, we did our best to remain true to our principles. We never lost sight that the essence of our struggle was love itself, and that was a real contribution to humanity."

Since the war years, from among the company of Engaged Buddhist leaders Thich Nhat Hanh has made probably the single greatest contribution to global thinking about peacemaking with his idea of "being peace." To make peace, he argues, it is necessary to "be peace." Nhat Hanh spent most of the years of the Vietnam War in the West, where he observed American peace demonstrations. He saw a great deal of anger and aggression in these demonstrations and said that they seemed to him like yet another war, this time between the pro-war and anti-war forces. He recognized that the anti-war protesters were sincere in their desire for the war in Vietnam to end but felt that they were going about it in entirely the wrong way. To him it is impossible to create a state of peace starting from a state of angry opposition to those with whom one disagrees. The means determine the ends; in order to make peace, one must do so in a peaceful way, building it step by step through peaceful actions emanating from a peaceful heart and mind. He sought to communicate to the West the principle of the Buddhist Struggle Movement: our enemies, he said, are hatred, inhumanity, anger, and ideology but not man. This principle of non-anger, or not opposing any individual or "side," has been difficult for mainstream Western political activists—raised to believe in the justifiability of "righteous" anger—to assimilate, but it has been rapidly embraced by a great number of activists whose motivation is religious, especially Christian pacifists, who feel considerable compatibility with this perspective.

For Nhat Hanh, healing the wounds of war and preventing the next war are also based upon "being peace." As is well known, many Vietnam veterans suffered psychological wounds that have lingered for decades. Nhat Hanh is very aware of this and regards it as an urgent matter to be redressed, not only for the sake of the veterans themselves, but for the sake of society as well. After a war, he says, remaining bombs must be defused. Those who have suffered through war have many bombs inside them, and these need to be defused as well. These "bombs," or psychological wounds from the war, are karmic seeds of pain, anger, and suffering; they are negative karmic seeds that, if left alone, will cause suffering for the one who bears them and for those around him when those bombs explode. It is no good to just leave them alone, for they are simply ripening, building up and coming closer to the time when they will bear painful fruit. They must be faced and defused. To help with the defusion Nhat Hanh has offered many retreats specifically for Vietnam War veterans.

It might seem strange that a Vietnamese should offer healing retreats for American veterans, but it is consistent with Nhat Hanh's teaching about the way to deal with suffering. Never turn away from suffering, he says, but face it, be with it, in a state of mindfulness. Veteran Claude Thomas, who was carrying profound psychological wounds from the war, speaks of his shock when he first encountered Nhat Hanh at a retreat. He says that he never knew the Vietnamese in any way other than as the enemy. Seeing Nhat Hanh, he suddenly realized that he was not his enemy. And he just started to cry.

American veterans of the Vietnam War did not receive a hero's welcome upon their return home. Many received contempt and blame. If contempt and blame did not come from others, many carried considerable self-contempt and self-blame for the lives they took and survivor's guilt for outliving their comrades. They were unable to move on in their lives. The Buddhist nonjudgmentalism discussed in chapter 2 has been critical to the effort to heal these wounds. "Why keep the guilt only for yourselves?" asks Nhat Hanh, adding that the entire society was to blame—the president, the Congress, the people; "You are only the hand ordered to do the act." For Nhat Hanh, the interdependent, multiple causes of the war—including Cold War ideology— were all responsible for the war; it was a massive playing out of karmic causes and conditions that swept all the participants along with it. See that, and the self-blame begins to loosen up. Moreover, he says, don't remain stuck in the past. One veteran told Nhat Hanh the story of how he and his comrades had been ambushed by men disguised as Buddhist monks, who killed several of his friends and wounded him. He decided to retaliate by leaving a bomb hidden where it would be sure to be found. A group of children found the bomb and died in the explosion. The veteran carried the guilt for decades. Nhat Hanh told him there was nothing he could do about what had happened in the past. But he could do something now to save the lives of children who were dying right now in the world. He could return to the present and do something to save their lives.

Nhat Hanh teaches veterans the same practices that he teaches everyone: to live in the present moment, develop mindfulness, and cultivate the seeds of loving-kindness and compassion that we all have within. These, he says, will give us inner peace and the ability to live a happy and constructive life. One practice particularly suited to Vietnam veterans can be mentioned. At a retreat for veterans in Washington, D.C., Nhat Hanh led a walking meditation at the Vietnam War Memorial. A walking meditation is a slow walk in a state of mindfulness. In the traditional practice, one focuses one's attention on the physical sensations of walking. Here the focus was on the Memory Wall. Mindfulness brings all of one's attention to whatever one is focusing on in the present moment. If the practice is done correctly, one should be very alert, making no judgment or commentary but taking everything in with nothing to mediate or soften what comes in. One is mindful also of one's involuntary response to what one is experiencing. Thus whatever grief, guilt, or anger one feels upon seeing the names of the dead on the Memory Wall, one consciously perceives it without commentary or judgment, without resistance or denial, but with acceptance and with loving-kindness toward oneself for whatever pain this experience calls up. Every time such feelings come up and one can accept them gently and without judgment, their power is lessened. This is a practice for healing.

Sri Lanka

Violent ethnic conflict between the Sinhalese majority and the Tamil minority has killed some sixty-five thousand people in Sri Lanka since 1983, not only in pitched battles between opposing armies, but also

stop the killing first and then work on all the issues that need to be resolved. The difficulty is that violence is self-perpetuating, as the law of karma states that it must be: those who have been harmed often want to retaliate and cause the other side harm; karmic seeds of hatred that have been planted will bear fruit in acts of hatred. In order to put an end to this cycle, Sarvodaya has given a great deal of attention to removing popular support for the violent acts committed by both the government and the Tamil Tigers. It urges three kinds of action in order to achieve that end.

First, it urges all Sri Lankans to eliminate violence from their own hearts and actions. One way of doing so is through participating in peace meditations. A program of large, public, Sarvodaya-sponsored peace meditations began in 1999 with a massive peace walk and peace meditation in Colombo that drew 170,000 people. Since then, many other large public peace walks and meditations have been held throughout Sri Lanka. In 2002, 650,000 people gathered in Anuradhapura for a Sarvodaya-sponsored peace meditation, possibly the largest public meditation ever held. Peace meditations held since then have attracted up to half a million people. All together, over two million people have meditated with Sarvodaya—10 percent of the total population of the country! These peace meditations, and many more like them, focus on cultivating loving-kindness *(mettā)* and can be contrasted with the peace rallies with which we are more familiar in the West. The latter tend to consist of many speeches, sometimes angry; cheers accompany particularly clever or powerful remarks. People carry placards, banners, and effigies stating their demands or ridiculing those they oppose. At the Sarvodaya peace meditations, people are asked to prepare in advance by dedicating themselves to basic moral principles, such as not harboring thoughts of killing but instead extending loving-kindness to all beings, and they are asked to refrain from language expressing hatred or blame. The peace walks and meditations are conducted in silence. There are no banners or placards other than the name boards of participating organizations; there are no speeches or lectures. People walk in three rows, wearing white clothing devoid of ornamentation, performing a walking meditation. When all are gathered at the meditation site, for one hour they practice meditation on the breath and loving-kindness meditation, directing this loving-kindness to all, without regard to ethnic differences. They then direct their minds toward the spiritual uplifting of all, without regard to religious differences. The assembly closes with ten minutes in which the various religious dignitaries present, representing all the major Sri Lankan religions, give their blessings to the crowd and to the work for peace. Participants disperse in the same manner in which they gathered, in silence. The entire event lasts about three hours.

The immediate goal of the peace meditation is to eliminate violence from the hearts and actions of the participants. Of course one meditation, however large and dramatic, cannot do that alone, but participants are asked to continue this meditation regularly at home. If this regular meditation can help give individuals more inner peace, Sarvodaya believes that it will help them to reorient their whole way of thinking in a more peaceful direction; the ultimate result will be more peaceful actions as well.

Once participants have begun developing their own personal peacefulness, they are asked to spread that peacefulness around. As the second and third actions for removing popular support for violent acts, Sarvodaya urges participants to ask everyone they know (2) to stop violence and to stop supporting violence and (3) to speak against violence

Sarvodaya Peace Meditation. Source: Sarvodaya Shramadana.

and for peace at every opportunity. In other words, when they hear a friend, family member, or co-worker (among others) make an insulting or angry remark about another ethnic group, they are expected to challenge that remark; when they hear someone voicing satisfaction that another ethnic group has suffered attack, they are expected to challenge that remark. Participants are asked to educate the media to support peace work rather than to ridicule it. These actions are part of an effort to change the culture of Sri Lanka from one that is supportive of hostility and violence—one in which it is commonplace to vocally support hostility against an ethnic group that is not one's own—to one that regularly expresses confidence that the war can be ended and a peaceful sharing of the island can be achieved. This goal cannot be achieved if people don't believe in it. Moreover, violent attacks from either the government or the Tamil Tiger side can continue only if they have popular support from their respective publics. If a popularly elected government pursued violent policies of which the public strongly disapproved, it would soon be voted out of office. Even a guerrilla army relies upon the public to hide, feed, and arm them. If public support for the warring factions could be removed, it would end the violence. The peace meditations demonstrate just how much the people of Sri Lanka want peace. Sarvodaya's ability to bring one-tenth of the population out to publicly demonstrate a desire for peace is an impressive showing that the politicians and extremist elements cannot miss.

All of these are only the first steps of the process to achieve a cease-fire. A cease-fire is just an opportunity to pause the violence, not a cure for it. Once a cease-fire has been achieved, one can begin to address the underlying causes of the conflict, and if the underlying causes can be dealt with, the cease-fire may become lasting. Therefore, the Sarvodaya peace program states that after a cease-fire has been obtained, Sri Lankans should take up the two primary causes of violence that have been identified.

Beginning with the problem of ethnic hatred, Sarvodaya asks all parties to work toward healing, reconciliation, and inclusivity for all communities. On the basis of its decades of nonsectarian development work, Sarvodaya is the only group with a national presence that is trusted by all the ethnic groups of Sri Lanka. All ethnic groups in the villages where it works participate in its efforts and have equal voice. Decisions are made by consensus. Work projects mix together members of different ethnic groups. Celebrations share prayers, music, and skits from all groups, with minorities given the honor of going first. Moreover, Sarvodaya has long been active in villages in all parts of the country, including the Tamil-dominated areas, and has drawn its leadership from both the Tamil and Sinhalese populations.

In more recent years, since turning its focus toward ending the war, Sarvodaya has developed new programs to heal ethnic hated. One of the most dramatic is its "1,000 Village Link-Up" program, which matches villages in Tamil and Muslim areas in the north and east of the island with villages in the more prosperous Sinhalese south. Thousands of people from the south volunteered to work in Tamil-Muslim areas during 2002, giving their time, labor, project materials (for the rehabilitation of [among other things] houses, wells, tanks, toilets, schools, and places of religious worship—churches, mosques, and temples), and their friendship in an effort to build amity and understanding by working together on a common project and in this way to build a lasting peace on a solid foundation of trust, understanding, and goodwill. These thousands of people trying to build peace are a good example of what Ariyaratne calls his Sarvodaya "army," which he believes to be a stronger force than either the government or Tamil Tiger armies.

In fact, a cease-fire agreement was reached in 2002. Many outside observers credited Sarvodaya with creating an atmosphere that made it possible to reach that agreement. Several years of relative peace ensued. Sadly, late in 2005 serious violence broke out again. Sarvodaya believes that the cease-fire was viewed as a cessation of hostilities rather than as a temporary halt in violence; people failed to take the critical opportunity that the cease-fire provided to eliminate the underlying causes of the violence. Since those underlying causes remained, violence eventually broke out again.

With the renewal of violence, Sarvodaya began a substantial new peace initiative called the Last Mile for Peace: Sarvodaya Initiative for a People's Constitution. This program was multifaceted. The first step consisted in consultations among all ethnic, religious, and civil groups about the needs, hopes, and visions of their communities. The input from these consultations became the basis for a draft of a "Common Vision," publicized from June 2007. The draft vision statement attempts to highlight the unity and shared values among all the Sri Lankan people, pointing out that everyone wants a life free of violence and a government that is fair and under the control of the people. It asserts that it is not the differences in religion, ethnicity, and regional identity per se that cause violence but inequality in power. The proposed solution to this problem is not for one set of elites to take power from another set of elites, but a devolution of power from the elites, who do not really represent the people, to the people themselves. Sarvodaya hopes that this vision statement will be debated all over the country.

Since the early 1990s Ariyaratne has been arguing for a national governance system without political parties and without a strong, centralized government, both of which he believes have had a negative influence on postcolonial social and political life in Sri Lanka. In their place he advocates a system in which Sri Lankan villages are self-governing and autonomous—in effect, small republics unto themselves—and organized into a federation with limited powers and operating by consensus. For Sarvodaya, village autonomy would provide the institutional structure most fitting for each ethnic community's wish to arrange the conditions of life according to their own preference. In Sarvodaya's view, there is no reason not to do so; a central government that forces all people to live according to a single vision of the good life is tyrannical in and of itself. This, then, is Sarvodaya's ultimate solution to the country's civil war: to transform Sri Lanka into a federation of participatory democracies.

These efforts, in brief, are Sarvodaya's way of working for peace in Sri Lanka. Violence continues as of this writing, and the outcome of the ethnic political struggle is unpredictable. Sarvodaya continues to be a major player in shaping events; it is creative and flexible in its response to events but is also pro-active in its efforts to build peace from the ground up.

Cambodia

Healing the wounds of war in Cambodia has been the lifework of Maha Ghosananda and the Dhammayietra that he instituted, an annual, month-long walk for peace. The Dhammayietra began in Cambodia after the fall of the Khmer Rouge, when the country was in shock and near collapse from that genocidal rule (1975–1979), which left between one and over two million dead (out of a population of seven million). Such numbers boggle the mind. The Khmer Rouge had targeted Buddhist monks for killing, so the Sangha (community) of monks was all but wiped out. Maha Ghosananda, who had been training in Thailand during the Khmer Rouge years, returned to Cambodia to work for healing and reconciliation.

In 1992 Maha Ghosananda and his assistants organized the first Dhammayietra. A *yietra* is a pilgrimage or spiritual walk, and "Dhamma" is Pali for "Dharma." "Dhammayietra" is often translated as "peace walk," a walk in peace for peace. The purpose of the first Dhammayietra was to accompany some of the refugees returning home from the refugee camps on the Thai border. With a marked lack of support from the Thai and Cambodian governments and the hostility of the UN High Commission for Refugees, the Dhammayietra set out from the Thai border with over a hundred refugees. Their final destination was the Cambodian capital, Phnom Penh, three-quarters of the way across the country. As they walked, participants came upon relatives they hadn't seen for ten or twenty years and whom they had no way of knowing whether they were still alive. Along the way, people spontaneously lined up for water blessings from the monks—a traditional practice on auspicious occasions—in order to feel a connection with what was to them a holy procession. The mere sight of the Dhammayietra supported the people's hope that peace was possible and human decency might return. Many people spontaneously joined the Dhammayietra as it came through their villages, and by the time it reached the capital a month later, it was twelve kilometers long.

Originally only one Dhammayietra had been organized, but with the success of the first walk and the continued lack of peace in the country, a second was planned. It was held the following year imme-

place. When Maha Ghosananda returned to Cambodia from Thailand, though the Khmer Rouge no longer held national power, the country was not yet at peace. Four major factions were still battling each other militarily and struggling politically. It was not possible to work for both peace and political accountability. Maha Ghosananda's priority was peace. He had access to leaders of all four factions and helped to bring them together to work out reconciliation. The Dhammayietra made essential contributions to the pacification of the remote areas of the countryside and to the process that made an elected government possible. These steps had to come first. In the new government, former Khmer Rouge leaders held important positions. It was impossible to entirely remove them from power without a renewed onset of political and military battles. In addition, to this day corruption pervades Cambodian society, including its judiciary. Neither politically nor judicially has it been possible to get fair and objective trials that people can and will trust. In such circumstances, truth commissions cannot function well, and the verdicts of trials carry little weight. It is difficult to know what is best in such a situation. In fact, there has been some progress: an international genocide tribunal has begun work in Cambodia; it handed down its first indictment against a top Khmer Rouge leader on July 31, 2007, almost three decades after the fall of the Khmer Rouge and after many of its leaders have died of natural causes.

Since they began, the walks have continued annually, in different areas and with different focal concerns each time, even after Maha Ghosananda became too old and infirm to participate and even after he died in 2007. Since the elections, the focal concerns of the walks have included such problems as land mines, domestic violence, and deforestation. However, much remains to be done in Cambodia. Even the bones of the dead remain stacked in piles, awaiting cremation. Cambodians believe that until the bones are cremated, the dead are not at rest, but, tragically, even the political unity and will to get this task done is not yet present in Cambodia.

Since the death of Maha Ghosananda no comparable leader has emerged in the Cambodian Sangha. Though monks still participate in the walks, the Dhammayietra is now, surprisingly, organized by a laywoman, Sy Vorn. Taking the corruption and moral bankruptcy of the country as the most pressing issue, she has focused the Dhammayietra upon teaching the five precepts, urging people to abide by the precepts, and showing how they apply to everyday life. In Buddhist terms, this is like teaching the ABCs; to learn the precepts is the very first and most elementary step in Buddhist practice. This approach is perhaps a fitting legacy to Maha Ghosananda, whose motto was "Slowly, slowly, step by step. Each step is a prayer."

tain ways of earning a livelihood, while they might not violate the laws of the state, are inherently immoral inasmuch as they cause suffering to others and so should be avoided. Such forms of livelihood, he taught, include any trades that involve weapons, poisons, drugs, alcohol, or any trade in human beings or animal flesh.

In addition, the Buddha gave quite specific advice on the disposition of wealth, counseling members of the laity that if they had sufficient wealth, they should see to the reasonable comfort of themselves and their families and then use any excess in generous sharing with others, in investment in their businesses, in prudent savings against possible future misfortunes, and in giving to deserving religious persons. Thus a layperson's wealth, even wealth that exceeds one's daily needs, is by no means a bad thing as long as it is put to proper use. What does earn the Buddha's censure is the miser who, in hoarding his wealth, causes himself suffering and deprives others as well. In order to be able to treat wealth as one should, the Buddha points out, one must cultivate a mental state such that one will not be grasping of what one has acquired, cling to it, obsess and worry about it, hoard it, or consider it an end in itself.

To cultivate the proper state of mind with respect to wealth, the Buddha counsels laypersons to develop moderation and contentment. Food is essential to health and well-being, but overeating makes one sick. Similarly one can desire all kinds of foods that are not conducive to good health; desires are endless. Here the Middle Path applies: one eats to satisfy needs and to promote overall well-being. One can certainly enjoy the food one eats, but one should cultivate contentment with the moderate consumption that fulfills one's needs and promotes health and avoid the effort to satisfy endless desires. This principle applies to all forms of consumption; the constant principle that runs through the Buddha's teachings is that everything we consume is a means, not an end, and to follow the Middle Path of moderation with contentment.

The Buddha's teachings on economics are linked to a social teaching as well. The Buddha taught that poverty is a terrible form of suffering that should not be allowed to exist. It is the duty of the government, he declared, to care for those who are impoverished and see that their needs are met. For example, in the *Cakkavatti Sīhanāda Sutta*, the sutta on the "wheel-turning" monarch (the ideal Buddhist king), the Buddha instructs the king that he should do all things according to Dhamma, protect the people and animals of the kingdom, "let no crime prevail in [his] kingdom, and to those who are in need, give property." Not only should poverty be assuaged, but also it should be regarded as the fundamental cause of crime and social disorder and therefore prevented. In the same sutta, the Buddha teaches a fable in which a king's failure to prevent poverty results in a cascade of negative social consequences. "Thus, from the not giving of property to the needy, poverty became rife, from the growth of poverty, the taking of what was not given increased, from the increase of theft, the use of weapons increased, from the increased use of weapons, the taking of life increased." The moral of the story is that for the sake of peace and social order, rulers should see to it that poverty never arises.

The Engaged Buddhists

Engaged Buddhist leaders derive the following economic principles from the teachings of the Buddha as they apply those teachings to the current economic conditions and problems of the world: (1) Economic issues are important. People are psychophysical organisms. Therefore Buddhists are mistaken if they imagine that the proper concern of their religion is with only the spiritual well-being of individuals and not their physical well-being. The spiritual and the material are interdependent; one cannot be separated from the other. Moreover, simple compassion compels one to help those who suffer from severe poverty.

(2) In applying the Middle Path to economic issues, the Engaged Buddhists conclude that Buddhism is not a friend of poverty, but neither can excessive wealth in the hands of a few be justified. Ariyaratne interprets this principle to mean that the correct economic goal for the development of a poor country is certainly not to pursue policies that further enrich the small number of wealthy people, but to look to the needs of the poor by building a "no poverty, no affluence" society in which everyone's basic needs are met.

(3) The dominant economic model promotes endless economic

growth, but this is not realistic; the planet's resources are finite. The correct goal is not growth but sufficiency. Moreover, the endless effort to fulfill all of one's cravings is doomed to failure, as the early life of the Buddha demonstrates; humans can never find satisfaction through material consumption. Therefore, rather than promoting consumption, Buddhism should promote contentment and moderation.

(4) Regarding economic theory, there is no unity. The Asian Engaged Buddhists—who work in undeveloped countries and are therefore in a position to take a view more open to many possibilities—generally have concluded that neither capitalism nor communism can serve as an economic theory compatible with Buddhism. Capitalism will not do because it inherently promotes endless consumption—the more the better. This is seen as reinforcing the insatiability of our desires and promotes greed. While there is a certain natural sympathy for socialism among the Asian Engaged Buddhists—with its attention to the good of all—communism will not do because of its historical record of brutal tyranny and hostility to religion. In particular, Buddhism in Asia has suffered horrific attacks from communism in China, Tibet, and Cambodia, with millions directly killed by Communist policies in each country; in Vietnam, Buddhism has been severely suppressed by Communist power. Most Engaged Buddhists are understandably extremely wary of communism.

In practice, in less developed countries in Asia, Engaged Buddhists generally promote a kind of humanistic socialism whose basic premise is that economics should be concerned with the welfare of the many. In the West, Engaged Buddhists generally take one of two approaches. The first is to criticize consumerism, denigrate capitalism, and encourage people to practice moderate consumption. The second is to take the world as they find it and look for ways to work within the established capitalist system and encourage businesses to behave in more socially responsible ways.

When working with extremely poor people, Asian or Western, Engaged Buddhists work very energetically to help them lift themselves out of poverty. When working with very wealthy people, they preach moderation and restraint. What makes such different approaches consistent is that they are both applying the Middle Path. One possible exception to this pattern is the Soka Gakkai, an Engaged Buddhist group of the Nichiren school. Many other Engaged Buddhists criticize the group precisely because it seems to support materialistic attitudes, even among the well-to-do. However, the members of Soka Gakkai see themselves as accepting people where they are—initially embracing people's materialistic attitudes if that's what they come with, but gradually transforming these attitudes such that people become less materialistic and more concerned with the welfare of others.

The economic situation of the world today is fundamentally different from the way it was during the time of the Buddha. At that time, compassion and modest means were all one needed to deal with poverty and economic issues: when a hungry man passed by, he was fed. But such an approach is no longer sufficient. Thanks to modern electronic communications, we now know about the hunger of people all over the world—the 1.2 billion people who, according to the World Bank, live in absolute poverty. This figure is 24 percent of the world's population, 46 percent of the population in sub-Saharan Africa. We see images of these people on television, on the Internet, and on magazine covers. Compassion wants to feed them all, but wisdom knows that fundamental changes both in the consciousness of the wealthy and in global economic structures will be necessary for this to happen.

An awareness that fundamental changes must take place leads the Engaged Buddhists to advocate for economic justice—specifically for a fair distribution of wealth so that no one lives in abject poverty and no one goes hungry. Even soft-spoken leaders like the Dalai Lama grow quite passionate over the plight of the desperately poor and declare it to be completely immoral for some to live in profligate luxury while others scavenge on garbage heaps. Moreover, just as the Buddha saw a link between poverty and crime, so the Engaged Buddhists see a link between global economic imbalances and violence: as the global poor learn how much their lives are unlike the lives of the global wealthy, resentment and anger grow and may be expressed in violence. Neither the suffering of the poor nor the sowing of seeds of global resentment are tolerable from the Engaged Buddhists' perspective. Much of their response has been to make the Western world aware of the problem of poverty and to urge restraint in the Western lifestyle and attention to the needs of the global poor. Dr. A. T. Ariyaratne and the Sarvodaya Shramadana, as we shall see, have gone the farthest in actually challenging global economic patterns and experimenting with alternatives.

Anti-Consumerism

Thai Engaged Buddhist layman Sulak Sivaraksa and American Engaged Buddhists Stephanie Kaza and David Loy are representative of the Engaged Buddhist concern with consumerism. Their thinking on this subject, though developed in distinct ways by each, is based upon the same principles. Consumerism in their view is closely tied to capitalist economics—specifically the tenet of the latter that holds that economies must continually grow in order to be healthy. In order for an economy to grow, people must continually buy the goods that the economy produces. Consumerism is the ideology that supports continual economic growth by promoting consumption. Consumption is promoted of course by the incessant advertising to which people in the developed world are subjected, but according to these thinkers, it is also promoted more subtly by the ideology of consumerism, which teaches us to identify ourselves as "consumers," to understand our lives as good if we have many possessions, and to conceive the purpose of our lives as the acquisition of more and more things. We commodify more and more of the things around us, thinking, for example, that a wedding or a burial needs to cost thousands of dollars or that (if we are Buddhist) we should fill our homes with Zen alarm clocks and Tibetan rugs. Our economic theory, in turn, supports this view by persuading us that the value of an object is the same as its cost. It leaves out of the equation what it can neither commodify nor quantify, such as clean air or harmonious neighborhood relations. These things literally do not count as economists make their calculations.

Sulak, Kaza, and Loy agree that consumerism dominates the developed world and is pushing deeply and quickly into the developing worlds. The consequences include the global North consuming a greatly disproportionate share of the Earth's resources, resulting in ruinous debt for many people. The developing world hastens to catch up, creating a great deal of debt there as well. In both areas heavy consumption takes a heavy toll on the natural world, with serious pollution, global warming, and rapid depletion of natural resources—through, for example, the heavy consumption of oil in the West and the rapid disappearance of forests in Thailand. Globally consumerism is creating a monoculture in which the products of the West are sold to the entire world, becoming part of the culture everywhere. Traditional cultures are finding it difficult to compete and are steadily losing ground to Western, commodified culture.

From a Buddhist point of view it is easy to see consumerism in terms of the first two Noble Truths. *Duḥkha,* the fundamental dissatisfaction with life that afflicts humanity, manifests as a constant craving for something better, something more. Consumerism hits us right here, in this our weak point, telling us that we are right to want something more, and advertising suggests endless possibilities for something that just might satisfy us. Yet somehow it never does. Nevertheless, we seem to act on a kind of blind faith, contrary to all our experience, that next time, the next product will satisfy our craving. Sulak and Loy call consumerism a "religion," with malls as the places of worship and advertising the liturgy. But this is a false religion that can never satisfy us.

In responding to the problem of consumerism, Engaged Buddhists have largely emphasized working on the personal level, using education, meditation, and work with precepts to change individual attitudes and behaviors. An example can be seen in Thailand, where economists, aware that consumerism is necessary for a growth economy, labeled Buddhism (since it promotes contentment and moderation) a regressive force hindering the development and modernization of the country. The Thai government took these economists' views to heart and for a time prohibited the monks from preaching the traditional value of contentment, so intent was it on removing obstacles hindering development. Thai so-called "development monks"—who oppose Westernized development—countered with renewed and even more pointed Dharma teachings on the virtues of contentment and moderation. These monks know the plight of rural villagers, among whom it is not uncommon to have gone so heavily into debt that they may be on the verge of losing their land to the banks that have loaned them money. The development monks encourage such villagers to take religious vows that they will resist consumerism, decrease their expenditures, and donate the money saved to a village savings group that will pay off their debts before the banks foreclose. These same monks also sometimes take villagers to the local graveyard to perform a traditional graveyard meditation on the impermanence of human life. They hope that reflecting on the transience of life and the inevitability of death will give the villagers "spiritual immunity" from the pull of consumerism, bringing home to them its hollowness and insufficiency.

In the West, Engaged Buddhist and meditation teacher Elias Amidon has taken students for a day-long walking meditation in the Rockies and the next day has taken the same group to a local mall to do another walking meditation in mindfulness. Amidon and his students report an enhanced awareness of the way in which the vast and attractive displays of goods work on their minds, and they are able to observe their own nascent responses to such stimuli. They have found the mall meditation to be genuinely disturbing for the clarity with which it declares what our society values.

Working with precepts is another popular approach in Engaged Buddhists' efforts to control consumerism. This can be done in a traditional or a more innovative way. The traditional approach, often used by Asian monks working with rural laypeople, emphasizes the precepts as external restraints. One who has agreed to be restrained by the five lay precepts would have to avoid alcohol and drugs, sexual stimulants, and things that harm oneself or others. These restraints do not address the entire range of consumerism, but they make a very significant start.

For his part, Thich Nhat Hanh has also been strongly emphasizing the five precepts in his teaching tours over the last few decades, urging all of his many followers to take them. His approach to the precepts is innovative: the precepts are understood as mindfulness practices rather than external restraints, and their meanings are considerably broadened. His restatement of the fifth precept—traditionally an invitation to avoid intoxicants—invites practitioners to be mindful of everything they consume, be it physically or mentally. Practitioners are invited to vow to ingest only things that preserve peace, well-being, and joy in their bodies and minds and to observe a diet that avoids all intoxicants and toxins, whether from food, drink, and drugs or from television, music, movies, and publications (among other things). That is, one isn't vowing to avoid all television programs, for example, but only those that are considered toxic.

It is helpful to remember that work with precepts, whether in the traditional or more innovative form, does not stand alone as a simple negation but is taken on as one part of a larger spiritual life in which one is also perhaps developing inner peace and contentment or developing compassion—that is, developing something positive that can take the place of what one is eliminating from one's life. One also does not practice alone; one is responsible to one's community for maintaining the vows that one has taken; the community, in turn, has many people who have taken up a similar practice and thus serve as a support for the practice.

Sarvodaya Shramadana

Dr. A. T. Ariyaratne and the Sarvodaya Shramadana movement of Sri Lanka have achieved the most by far in the area of economics of any Engaged Buddhists. Their accomplishments encompass both a radical and visionary rethinking of economic theory and extensive practical accomplishments in development and economic empowerment in the villages of Sri Lanka. Sarvodaya is now active in over fifteen thousand of Sri Lanka's approximately twenty-four thousand villages. In some of the most active villages, its activity constitutes almost an alternative grassroots self-government.

Sarvodaya has for almost fifty years served Sri Lankans as a development organization. Oddly perhaps for a development organization, it emphasizes the well-established Buddhist values of Middle Path, moderation and contentment. Because material needs are means and not ends and because the true end is a spiritual condition that includes contentment with what is sufficient, Sarvodaya opposes the usual economic assumption that continuous, unending economic growth is both necessary and good. It is convinced that such growth is simply unsustainable—as noted above, the Earth and its resources are finite;

they have a limit that we simply have to respect. Moreover, the idea of continual growth is based upon the practice of trying to fulfill all of humankind's desires and leads inevitably to the instigation and promotion of still more desires, as businesses try to "grow" their markets and compete through advertising for a greater market share. Such efforts are completely antithetical to Buddhism's views as expressed in the Four Noble Truths and the teaching of the Middle Path. Desires are the foundation of *duḥkha,* and they are inherently insatiable. For the sake of eliminating *duḥkha* and replacing it with contentment, we need to stop chasing after the fulfillment of our desires. How, then, can there be such a thing as a Buddhist development organization? Is that not oxymoronic? Ariyaratne resolves this very simply by stating that Sarvodaya is interested in helping Sri Lankans meet their needs, not their greeds. Needs, however, are needs and must be met.

Sarvodaya is radically different from other development organizations, which focus exclusively on economic development, narrowly defined in terms of the development of wealth, the production of goods, and the expansion of employment. Sarvodaya's idea of development is much broader because it is trying to achieve development in the Buddhist sense of total human development or what it calls "awakening"—the awakening of the villagers as individuals and the awakening of the village as a whole, these two kinds of awakening being interdependent.

Probably the most fundamental affirmation of Buddhism is its endorsement of human development. This endorsement is based on the Buddhist idea of the human being. In Buddhism we are by nature beings in process. We are not beings who "are" in a static sense, but beings who are *becoming.* Moreover, each one of us has the potential of becoming something great, something that goes beyond the ordinary mode of human being: we have the potential to become Buddhas. Sarvodaya envisions spiritual development at the apex of a hierarchy of human needs, all of which it embraces within its understanding of what is involved in human development and all of which are therefore within the embrace of its development programs. Sarvodaya has identified ten basic human needs that its programs attempt to help people meet. Material needs are served as necessary parts of this greater whole and as means to the greater end of spiritual development. The ten basic human needs, arranged loosely in a hierarchy, are the following:

1. A clean environment
2. A clean and adequate water supply
3. Simple clothing
4. Balanced food
5. Simple housing
6. Basic health care
7. Simple communication facilities
8. Minimum energy
9. Total and continuing education for all
10. Cultural and spiritual development

With this list Sarvodaya is trying to identify in concrete terms what is required for an impoverished person—who is chronically hungry, malnourished, and in poor health; has low self-esteem because he cannot provide for his family; has no hope because everyone else he knows has always lived the same way; sees nothing around him with which to better himself; drinks as much as possible to forget his despair; behaves sullenly and with occasional violence because of his resentment over his lot in life; and who nonetheless has the potential of becoming a Buddha—to become a Buddha. This list is the elaboration and concretization of the Buddha's understanding that a hungry man must eat before he can listen to the Dharma. It then guides the Sarvodayans in their effort to make available all the necessary supports for such a person to grow into his potential of Buddhahood.

By no means does Sarvodaya imagine that this process involves giving handouts. Quite the opposite. One of the keys to Sarvodaya's programs is that they are all based upon self-help (as is the practice of Buddhism, at least as taught by the Buddha). This is a process of empowerment.

How does this empowerment function concretely? Sarvodaya typically begins its work in a village when its organizers are invited. They then organize a "family gathering," inviting the entire village to attend—men, women, and children and all ethnic and religious groups. At the family gathering, participants speak to each other using familial terms—for example, younger brother, older sister, and aunt—an approach that immediately begins to undercut divisions of ethnicity, religion, political affiliation, etc. The organizers invite the villagers to discuss the needs of the village and then decide together on a concrete project—such as building a road or a well—that they themselves can do together to improve the village for everyone. The decision should be reached by consensus.

Once a decision has been made, a work camp, or shramadana (which means "giving labor," with all the Buddhist connotations of the meritorious nature of giving), is organized. At the shramadana all the villagers are again invited to participate by giving their labor to the village as a whole. They work together in teams, and by the end, all who have participated know that they have with their own hands produced a valuable addition to the village. They did not wait for the government or experts or anyone else. That is empowering. They begin to see themselves as people who can do things. Thus, as we noted above, one of the favorite slogans in Sarvodaya is "We build the road, and the road builds us." The road building the villagers is actually the more important of the two; it contributes to the development of each participant and to the building of new relationships among the villagers.

A Shramadana—Building a Road. Source: Sarvodaya Shramadana.

It is noteworthy that the list of ten basic human needs begins with a clean environment, a concern that has been part of the Sarvodaya program from the beginning. Even though the major concern of the entire program is the development of human beings, this goal is not allowed to serve as a rationalization for any action that would harm the environment. The Sarvodayans are aware of the interdependence between humankind and the natural world and are not going to sacrifice the well-being of the natural world for some shortsighted perception of an imagined gain for humankind. Also noteworthy on the list is the ninth need, "total and continuing education for all." This item is also very much an expression of Sarvodaya's commitment to human development in the Buddhist sense. Education here is not conceived as a preparation for joining the workforce, nor does it end when one reaches adulthood. Education covers all aspects of human development throughout life—not only the learning of useful skills and preparation for effective participation in public life, but also learning for spiritual development. As for one's entering the workforce, Ariyaratne emphasizes that a healthy economy provides for full engagement, not full employment. In other words, just as a person should be learning throughout life in order to continue developing throughout life, so should a person be fully engaged with life throughout his or her lifetime. This engagement may or may not have any relation to earning wages.

The best way to understand the cultural needs identified in the tenth item on the list is to recognize that we are cultural beings. That is, a great part of what shapes our development both as individuals and as societies comes from our culture. Culture is therefore very important. Sarvodaya finds the traditional culture of Sri Lanka a far more wholesome influence on personal and social development than globalized Western culture, with its emphases on consumerism, individualism, a fast-paced lifestyle, hypersexuality, and violence (as found, for example, in Hollywood movies and popular music)—all values that feed those inherently insatiable desires and greeds that are the base of *duḥkha* and that are antithetical to the kind of development that Sarvodaya would like to see in Sri Lanka. Moreover, such a lifestyle is unreachable by the poor of undeveloped countries, and its promotion simply fuels frustration and resentment. In fact, both Ariyaratne and Sulak (along with many other Asian cultural leaders) search for ways to protect traditional culture against the barrage of globalized Western culture. In many ways traditional cultures are like endangered species. Like species on, say, an island, they may become overwhelmed when species from other places come to the island, reproduce rapidly, and crowd them out of their ecological niches. Traditional cultures as well may be overwhelmed when globalized Western culture encroaches because that culture is so appealing to materialistic cravings, because it is relentlessly and aggressively marketed, and because it carries the allure of the West, with its power and prestige. To preserve, enjoy, and cultivate traditional culture therefore is a very important—though difficult—task to both Ariyaratne and Sulak.

Sarvodaya's village programs grow in a natural way from their foundation in an initial shramadana work camp. Preparation for the work camp involves organizing a village into teams of mothers, children, youth, men, and elders that meet together and coordinate their contributions to the shramadana. When the camp is over, the groups may continue to meet, discussing their needs and determining what they themselves can do to meet those needs. Often the next development comes from the women, who decide that they want to organize a preschool, a need that is not met by the government and one that will serve the needs of the children while freeing the mothers to do other things. Both men and women may be given the opportunity to learn new skills, start a small business, or organize a cooperative to make goods that can then be sold. Sarvodaya helps in these efforts by supplying instructors to train villagers or by supporting individuals chosen by the village to get training at a Sarvodaya center. Sometimes materials and often credit are also supplied by Sarvodaya to get a new village business up and running—Sarvodaya has worked extensively and successfully with micro-credit to help villagers lift themselves out of poverty. Many cottage industries and small businesses have been started in Sri Lankan villages using this micro-credit, in areas such as baking, printing, textiles, woodworking, metal working, dairies, tea shops, and small groceries.

Sarvodaya developed its own village savings and micro-credit programs as an alternative to the commercial banks, which were not serving the needs of the very poor, whom they regard as too great a financial risk. The village banks begin by encouraging the villagers to save; those with savings are permitted to apply for loans. Whether a loan should be granted is determined by a committee of villagers chosen for the purpose. Recipients of loans can draw upon the advice of Sarvodaya advisers regarding agricultural methods or small business development and management techniques.

One of the hallmarks of Sarvodaya's approach draws upon the Buddhist awareness of interdependence. From the start, Sarvodaya has been aware that its goal of awakening villagers requires a multifaceted approach, reflected in the ten basic needs discussed above. Interdependence requires that after the most critical physical needs have been met, all the ten needs must be worked on simultaneously. Thus from the very beginning of Sarvodaya's presence in a village, the shramadana work camps incorporate cultural celebrations from all the ethnic groups present. They also incorporate spiritual development with prayers from all the religions present and loving-kindness meditations. They always involve shared meals to help build community. After the work camps, many villages move quickly to invite Sarvodaya programs that offer instruction in nutrition and help the villages to acquire basic health services and immunizations. Sarvodaya addresses needs for ongoing learning by providing a great variety of training, not only in practical skills such as agricultural production or skilled trades, but also in such areas as education, health care, and community organizing. In addition, Sarvodaya helps villages form marketing cooperatives to market their products. It provides access to legal and library services. Sarvodaya has formed extensive Shanti Sena (Peace Brigade) programs for nonviolent self-policing, crowd control, mediation, and conflict resolution. It has made available information technology—telephones, e-mail, and computers—and the training to use it to all its district centers.

It must be emphasized that Sarvodaya does not run any of these programs; the villages run them for themselves, with credit, instruction, and/or organizational help from Sarvodaya to help them get started. Thus Sarvodaya provides training for teachers and advice on curriculum for the preschools, but the schools are under village control, and they adapt the curriculum as they see fit. The banks and credit societies are entirely under the control of each village. From the beginning such control was understood as a means of empowering the villages and freeing the villagers from the economic control of the banks. The information technology was designed from the beginning as a means for the villages to communicate directly with one another, allowing them to form networks without recourse to any centralized systems outside their control. Together all of Sarvodaya's programs— the shramadana work camps, the preschools and training, the health and nutrition care, the self-banking micro-credit and small business incubation, the marketing cooperatives, the agricultural improvements, the strengthening of community ties within the villages, the spiritual development and cultural celebrations, the communications technology, and the self-policing—amount to a massive transfer of power from centralized elites external to a village (politicians, bankers) to the local, decentralized level of the village, which is progressively empowered and enabled to care for more and more of its own needs. Finally, when it has reached a certain level of development, a Sarvodaya village is expected to reach out to other villages to offer its neighbors the kinds of programs and development opportunities from which it has benefited, with no need for Sarvodaya staff to be involved. It is clear that Sarvodaya is not amassing power or control for itself but transferring it from centralized elites to the local level.

Sarvodaya's goals have focused upon the awakening of the individual and the village within Sri Lanka, but in the last few decades the organization has been more and more concerned with global awakening as well. For some time Sarvodaya has been exporting its ideas to groups in other underdeveloped countries. It receives visitors from all over the world—Asia, Africa, North America, and Europe—who stay for a week or a year to learn about Sarvodaya's approaches and take them back home. Sometimes Sarvodaya sends Sarvodaya workers back with the foreign teams to help train others and get programs started. Of course non–Sri Lankan groups are expected to adapt their programs to their own particular needs, cultures, and religions. The Sarvodayans would be delighted if their vision of a loose federation of autonomous, self-governing villages could include villages from countries outside of Sri Lanka as well.

Sarvodaya is by far the largest and most successful Buddhist movement devoted to economic development. However, there are other movements in other Asian Buddhist countries that use some of the same principles. In Thailand the "development monks," mentioned above, work, like Sarvodaya, on the rural village level, educating the local people on eco-friendly agricultural methods that have the double benefit of protecting the environment and keeping the people from the debt that accrues from jumping to mechanized, chemical-based, and Western hybrid-seed agriculture. They invite people to make their traditional donations to the temple not for the support of the temple itself but to fund rice banks (which provide rice at planting season) and buffalo banks (which provide water buffalo for plowing) or to fund community development projects. Since the money is given to the temple, people believe they earn the same merit as they would if the temple used the money for its own purposes, but these donations return to the village in the form of material help. Thai "development monks" represent a small minority of the Thai monkhood, however. They work individually and on the local level, with only an occasional sharing of ideas among themselves.

Glassman

American Zen master Roshi Bernie Glassman, like Ariyaratne, has devoted a good part of his life to helping the poor lift themselves out of poverty, in Glassman's case, working in Yonkers, New York, in a run-down industrial warehouse district that, at the time Glassman began working there, had the highest per capita rate of homelessness in the United States. Glassman has studied Ariyaratne's work and learned a great deal from him but is working in a very different environment. Living in the United States, he is not in the position of the Sarvodaya movement, which has a comparatively open situation due to the relative lack of development in Sri Lanka. Glassman must work within the constraints of the economic system of the United States, attempting to help the homeless and chronically unemployed raise themselves to a livable income level that they will be able to sustain. He therefore does not raise the kinds of fundamental questions that Ariyaratne raises about the pros and cons of capitalism and socialism. He takes the American economic system as a given and works within it, using capitalism and profit making to the end of helping the poor.

Learning from Ariyaratne, Glassman began by asking homeless people what they needed. He expected them to say that they needed jobs, but by asking and listening, he found that they needed child care first, as well as a way to receive mail and telephone calls. He recognized that the homeless knew what they needed better than he did, and he allowed himself to be led by those needs. He ties this principle to a well-known Zen story. When a student asked a Zen teacher what the highest teaching of Zen is, the teacher wrote "Attention." The student asked, "Isn't there something else?" "Yes," said the Zen master, and wrote "Attention" again. "Surely there is something more," said the student. "There is," said the teacher, who again wrote "Attention." The message now read, "Attention. Attention. Attention." This is the same principle of mindfulness that the Theravada teachers discuss, but expressed in a Zen, Mahayana idiom. If you want to do something right, the most important thing is to empty your mind of preconceptions about what is necessary and be present, in the present moment, with an open mind, open eyes, and open ears.

Another point on which Glassman agrees with Ariyaratne is the central importance of self-sufficiency, of empowering the poor to take care of their needs themselves. For Glassman this has meant that the poor need a way to get off of welfare and provide for themselves. He quotes the Chinese adage, "Instead of giving a hungry man a fish, teach him how to fish." Like Ariyaratne, Glassman has learned from experience the importance of remembering interdependence when one is involved in social action. As we have seen, the homeless couldn't begin to think about getting jobs until they had child care and a way of receiving mail and telephone calls. It turned out that they also needed training in life skills and communication skills. They needed alcohol and drug counseling and a very strict policy enforcing limits. They needed decent and affordable places to live. They needed jobs, and they needed the training to succeed in those jobs. There was no way to solve the problem without addressing all of these interdependent needs at once. In the end, Glassman did just that by creating the Greyston Mandala, a network of for-profit businesses and not-for-profit agencies serving the poor. The Mandala is made up of the following: the Greyston Bakery, a $6 million business that bakes gourmet desserts and especially targets homeless and poor people to hire and train; the Greyston Family Inn, which provides affordable and decent housing renovated and managed by the formerly homeless and low-income working families themselves; Issan House, a housing facility for people with HIV/AIDS; and the Maitri Center, a day health service for people with HIV/AIDS. Necessarily related programs include training, counseling, child care, after-school programs, and community gardens.

Like Ariyaratne and like the Buddha, Glassman has argued against students who told him he should set his sights higher and give spiritual lessons rather than worrying about creating jobs for people. He has told them that people have to be met where they are—if they're hungry, let them eat first; if they're homeless and cold, find them shelter. But like Ariyaratne, Glassman realizes that development doesn't stop there; spiritual needs are a necessary and interdependent part of the picture. The answer for Glassman comes in making sure that the work in which everyone is involved is a form of Right Livelihood.

Glassman has done some serious thinking about Right Livelihood. He embraces the teaching that earning a livelihood is a necessary means but not an end in itself. With Right Livelihood, one earns enough to sustain oneself and one's dependents and put some aside in reserve. In addition, for Glassman Right Livelihood has a spiritual dimension; it feeds us spiritually as well as materially. This does not mean pushing Buddhism, of course. For Glassman the bottom line for the spiritual dimension of Right Livelihood is that work should serve personal and spiritual growth, helping us to become less egocentric and more capable of working well within our interdependence with each other and with the Earth. This goal was incorporated into the workplace by having people work in teams that were paid according to how the entire team accomplished its work. Thus it was in everyone's

interest to help one another and work smoothly together. Right Livelihood for Glassman also includes ongoing learning and some kind of
social action or benefit to others.

Glassman's work raises some interesting issues. Capitalism and consumerism are widely censured in the Engaged Buddhist world, yet Bernie Glassman, by all accounts one of the most creative and successful of
the Western Engaged Buddhists, is up to his elbows in both. Clearly he
is not against making a profit. Nor as a "gourmet confectioner" can the
Greyston Bakery be said to be taking the anti-consumerist approach.
Glassman discusses both of these points in the context of Right Livelihood. A bakery was selected largely because its work is very labor
intensive, allowing the creation of jobs for many people. The work is
such that people can be trained in fairly short order. Greyston had
friends in the Zen world who ran a bakery and would help it get started
(the San Francisco Zen Center's Tassajara Bread Bakery). Finally, baking develops skills that are important in Buddhist spirituality: detailed
care, mindfulness, attention, and harmonious interaction. For Glassman making a good profit is part of Right Livelihood, as it allows the
bakery to employ more people and for that employment to be stable.
Just as Sarvodaya's motto is "We build the road, and the road builds
us," Greyston states on its Web site, "We don't hire people to make
brownies; we make brownies in order to hire people"—specifically
people considered "hard to employ."

In addition, there is an important outreach element to the bakery's
work. The Greyston Bakery has become a well-known and award-
winning role model for the not inconsiderable number of businesses
interested in the social responsibility of corporations—that is, those
who want their businesses to have an element of social activism or at
least to give something back to their communities. In reaching out to
businesses considering such a stance it is important to demonstrate
that corporate responsibility does not have to mean a loss of profitability. If Greyston were not profitable, it would not be of interest to
corporations who want to make a positive contribution to the world
but are not about to forego profitability. By embracing the American
cultural value of entrepeneurship and participating successfully in the

American economy, Greyston invites the American mainstream to change its behavior in a way that it might seriously consider.

As for consumerism, Greyston initially intended to make bread, which seemed wholesome and necessary, but it turned out that making pastries worked better for it. Bread has to be made at night and delivered in the day, and that routine divided the community into one group that slept at night and another that slept in the day. Glassman believes that such a division within the community does not make for Right Livelihood. In addition, if Greyston baked bread, it would face competition from very large national businesses, whereas it found an available niche in making pastries. Pastries were even more labor intensive than bread, which was an asset for hiring more people. The unwholesomeness of pastries was discussed, but Greyston finally decided that if it made pastries from all natural ingredients, that would be wholesome enough!

CHAPTER 6

Ecology

It is widely felt that there is a great compatibility between Buddhist principles—both concepts and values—and an ecological perspective. Some take this even farther, pointing to ways in which Buddhist thinking opens up new possibilities for ecological thinking. The Engaged Buddhists are among those who are pioneering the exploration of this new area.

The Teachings of the Buddha and the Mahayana

The concept of interdependence is the most important source in the Buddha's teachings of the often cited compatibility between Buddhism and an ecological perspective. This concept, also known as dependent origination, points out that everything comes into being through a process of causes and conditions. That which has been caused in turn causes and conditions other things. Existence is thus a great web of interdependence or mutual interpenetration in which it is incorrect to think of things in isolation from each other.

Things are immediately implicit in each other. Thich Nhat Hanh teaches this by holding up a sheet of paper and asking his students whether they can see in it the cloud, sun, and soil. In other words, the paper comes from the tree, and the tree could not exist without the rain from the cloud, the warmth from the sun, and the minerals from the soil. Through Right Understanding one immediately sees cloud, sun, and soil upon viewing a sheet of paper. The ecological and economic implications of this become clear when we consider, in classic Buddhist fashion, that the reverse is also true: perhaps if the soil is too polluted or the sun's warmth excessive from being trapped within the atmosphere, there will be no tree and no sheet of paper.

The possibility of there being no tree and no sheet of paper brings up a second crucially important teaching of the Buddha for an ecological perspective. If we were concerned only that there might be no sheet of paper, we would be concerned only with the instrumental value of the tree—that is, its value for humankind, the uses to which we could put it. In Buddhism one part of the view of nature does involve regarding the tree as having instrumental value. That is one of the implications of dependent origination: we constantly draw upon many things in order to live. An instrumental regard of nature is not bad; in fact, it is the source of a great deal of affection and esteem for the natural world in Buddhism. There is a great regard for the Bo tree, beneath which the Buddha attained enlightenment; the Buddha himself praised this tree, and its purported offspring are the sites of devoted pilgrimage. The forest in general has been highly regarded as the site within which forest monks wander; both the challenges and the resources that the forest itself and its denizens offer constitute the very stuff of the practice in this tradition, and, as we shall see, to be at home in the natural world—like a forest monk—is itself an important resource in an age such as ours, in which many people are estranged from nature. Moreover, Buddhist monasteries and temple grounds have often evolved into sites where animal and plant lives are protected and species are preserved, whether intentionally or circumstantially.

At the same time, in Buddhism things are *also* seen as having intrinsic value—that is, they have value in themselves, just as they are, with no reference to their usefulness for oneself and one's group. Intrinsic value is implied in Theravada teachings and further developed in some Mahayana and East Asian teachings. Certainly the teaching of no-self, fundamental to both Theravada and Mahayana, already implies the most important point: no one of us is the center of the universe. To see things always in an instrumental way—that is, to see things always in terms of their usefulness to oneself—is an egocentric perspective. In objective terms, it is simply not true that other things exist primarily for oneself or for humankind—that is, that their being is well understood if they are considered only in their relation to oneself. The fact that most of us think this way (usually subconsciously) is simply a manifestation of our fundamental ignorance. Buddhist practice is all about making this shift from an egocentric perspective to a more objective perspective, and thus it is all about shifting from a perspective that sees things always in terms of their instrumental value to one that recognizes both instrumental and intrinsic values. We should be able often to be free in our thinking from instrumental considerations and simply see things as they are in themselves; such a perspective is called *tathatā*, the "suchness" or "thusness" of things. In some Mahayana traditions, to see things in their thusness is a large part of the very definition of enlightenment.

Also fundamental to both Theravada and Mahayana is the recognition of animals as sentient beings—that is, beings that have awareness and can suffer. Humanity's kinship with the animal world is rather strong in Buddhism since both humans and animals are sentient beings, revolving together in repeated births throughout samsara. Thus we all have been born as animals many times in the past and may well be born as animals again; likewise, a being that is born as an animal in its present existence may well be a human next time. This understanding inculcates a certain feeling of closeness to the animal world, an awareness that we are not fundamentally different from animals. Perhaps this latent awareness is what allows Buddhism to recognize that animals, like us, are aware and have the capacity to suffer (an understanding that was flatly rejected in Western philosophy and science for some time). From the awareness that animals suffer it is a short step, in Buddhism, to the understanding that it is not good for animals to suffer and that humans should do what they can to avoid causing such suffering and to relieve it when it exists. Thus the first lay precept strongly urges us to avoid killing, harming, or causing suffering to any sentient being, any being capable of suffering, and this very much includes animals as well as human beings. The defining element in this thinking about nonharmfulness is the capacity to suffer—any suffering is bad, and therefore the precept pertains to any being that is capable of suffering. In this way Buddhism avoids "speciesism"—the assumption that membership in a certain species (the human) is the relevant distinction—in the foundation of its ethical thought, particularly as it applies to nonharmfulness. Therefore it is basic to Buddhist ethics to avoid harming animals and to have compassion for any being—human or animal—that suffers. A number of texts urge us to develop loving-kindness for all beings without distinguishing among those with two, four, many, or no legs or among those that swim, fly, crawl, or walk.

The view of nature as having intrinsic value is very much strengthened in Mahayana and East Asian forms of Buddhism. Mahayana thought strongly develops Buddhist nonduality with the teaching of emptiness, itself a development of the concepts of interdependence and impermanence. As the reader may recall from chapter 3, emptiness represents the recognition that interdependence is so strong that it is wrong to think of the world as made up of "things" at all. This interdependence is represented when Thich Nhat Hanh holds up the sheet of paper and asks if we can see the sun and the cloud in it. If the concept is taken to its logical and linguistic extreme, we recognize that there is no sheet of paper at all, in the sense that there is no independent thing there at all, just a temporary merging of processes that will soon move on to form other mergings. What is, is impermanent, changing from moment to moment; nothing is the same—nothing is "itself"—from one moment to the next. This way of thinking ultimately leads to the erasure of all "things" as such and consequently to the erasure of all boundaries between what we perceive as "things."

As a result, Mahayana Buddhism manifests a very thoroughgoing nondualism in its thought. One form of this nondualism is the recognition of nirvana and samsara as nondual, or not two. There is one reality: perceived with a deluded mind, it is samsara; perceived without delusion, it is nirvana. There can be, then, no sacred-profane duality, no real distinction between the two. Whatever one seeks, there is nowhere else to find it but right here and right now. Moreover, the bodhisattva's vow to return again and again to samsara, as well as the bodhisattva's manifestation of enlightenment within samsara, also undercuts the earlier duality between samsara and nirvana. Some forms of Mahayana virtually cease mentioning nirvana and refer only to enlightenment or awakening. It is important to recognize that in Theravada nirvana never was correctly understood as a place at all, much less a place different from the place of samsara, much less the physical planet Earth. However, in practice the fact that Buddhists experienced samsara in their incarnations on Earth and the fact that the Buddha, after his *parinirvāṇa* (the final death of an enlightened being) was not reborn on Earth led to an association between samsara and the Earth as a place in the Theravada tradition. It is this dualism that Mahayana philosophical developments eliminated, at least in theory.

As Buddhism moved into different countries, it always absorbed elements of local cultures and religions. Particularly significant for our purposes was Buddhism's absorption of elements of Daoism in China. Daoism greatly esteems nature as the Dao. In Daoism, Dao is the ultimate source of all life and is also fully manifest in the natural world and its processes. This particular and thoroughgoing nondualism makes impossible any dualism between the sacred and the profane in Daoism. Buddhism in China was felt to be a kindred spirit with Daoism, and thus ideas such as these were absorbed into it, to the extent that the term "Dao" was used to translate the Buddhist term "Dharma." The result was a sense in much of East Asian Buddhism (Buddhism found in China and the other East Asian countries) that nature manifests supreme reality—what Mahayana Buddhism calls the *Dharmakāya*. A good example of this is Japanese Zen master Dogen's "Mountains and Rivers Sutra," which refers to the mountains and rivers actualizing the Dao of Buddha, manifesting it in completeness. Another is the work of Chinese Buddhist poet Han Shan, who lauded Cold Mountain as a place of unbounded freedom, where the Dao could be found in the mists and peaks. Still others are the works of countless Zen poets and painters who have depicted enlightenment as the moon reflecting in the still waters of a pond or as the cherry blossom blooming in perfection and then falling without struggle from the tree.

Deep Ecology

All of the above is theoretical. How much effect do such ideas have on human behavior with respect to the natural world? In the modern world at least these ideas are making an impact by way of "deep ecology." Deep ecology is a branch of ecological thought and practice founded by Arne Naess, a philosopher who draws upon Spinoza, Gandhi, and Buddhism. Naess himself has said that one of the easiest ways into deep ecology, or "green" thinking, is from a starting point in Buddhism, and it is certainly true that many of the deep ecology ideas follow naturally from the ideas discussed above.

Two great themes of deep ecology sound virtually identical to core ideas of Buddhist thought. The first is the scientific understanding that all systems of life on Earth are interrelated and interdependent, an idea that parallels the root Buddhist idea of dependent origination. On this basis, one can reasonably conclude that anthropocentrism, a focus on humans as the central or most important point of existence, is a false belief and that we should let go of it. The second principle is what Naess calls "self-realization," by which he means identification with others or seeing something of oneself in others; it is the realization of a broader "self" that can become broader and broader until it includes all beings, all animals, all biota, all of the natural world. Clearly in its further reaches, this idea has much in common with the Buddhist teaching of no-self. On a more mundane level, it is the simple realization that humankind is a part of the Earth, not separate or separable from it.

Because it has this kind of foundation, deep ecology has at its base a spirituality very much like a core form of Buddhist spirituality. Buddhism works for deep ecology because Buddhism is nondualistic and nontheistic. Buddhist nondualism is based in the same kind of awareness of interdependence, resulting in the same kind of dethroning of humanity from the center of the universe that deep ecology suggests. Naess' self-realization and Buddhism's no-self are both not so much ideas as transformative experiences made possible and even necessary by this dethroning. They are nondualistic experiences that change one's way of perceiving and experiencing such that one no longer feels a separation between oneself and the world. One feels the world to be a part of oneself and oneself to be part of the world, with continuity rather than separation between the two. Moreover, without a transcendent God, there is nothing in Buddhism to trigger a fundamental sacred-profane dualism such as is common in theistic systems, in which God, the angels, heaven, and all things related to God are regarded as sacred while the Earth and its denizens are regarded as profane. Without a sacred-profane dualism, there is nothing to make one see the Earth and its inhabitants as less than or inferior to some-thing else. The Earth and its inhabitants are therefore worthy of all of one's love and a lifetime of one's hard work on their behalf (which is not separate from one's own behalf).

Engaged Buddhism and Deep Ecology: Four Major Leaders

It is fair to say that one of Engaged Buddhism's major contributions has been to the development of the thought and practice of deep ecology. Joanna Macy, John Seed, and Gary Snyder are all major deep ecologists who are either Engaged Buddhists or strongly Buddhist-influenced. Though Zen master and Engaged Buddhist Thich Nhat Hanh is not usually mentioned in connection with deep ecology, his teachings also support the ideas of this school.

Probably Thich Nhat Hanh's most important contributions to deep ecology have been in the teaching of mindfulness practices that help people to get in touch with their bodies and the natural world. As we have seen, deep ecology is partially based upon overcoming the expe-riential split between self and world. The first step in overcoming this split for someone who identifies his "self" with his thoughts and emo-tions is to inhabit his body with more conscious attention. Nhat Hanh, like any mindfulness teacher, encourages people to eat mindfully (without commentary or judgment, in rapt absorption in the present moment of experience) as an intentional practice, eating slowly and paying full attention to the sights, smells, tastes, and textures when, for example, peeling an orange, placing a section on the tongue, chew-ing it, and swallowing. He has adjusted the traditional mindfulness practice of walking meditation from one that focuses exclusively on the sensations of walking (focusing on the sensations on the bottom of one's feet) to one that allows the focus to shift to feeling the warmth of the sun on one's face, feeling the coolness of the breeze, closely looking at the trees one encounters, feeling the roughness of their bark, and listening to the sounds of the birds and insects. With this practice one gets more and more in touch not only with one's body and the world around one, but also with the seamless continuity of world and body that is present in sensory experience. Gradually this kind of practice weakens the feeling of separation between self and world until ultimately it may lead one to the awareness expressed in the title of one of Nhat Hanh's books, *The Sun My Heart*. This is the awareness that is free of the experiential sense of self that is based in the felt separation between self and world. In the state of awareness that Nhat Hanh is describing, one feels that the world is "my" body and the sun that gives warmth and animation to the world is "my" heart. This practice also puts one in touch with the condition of the natural world. Nhat Hanh suggests that if one is walking mindfully, one doesn't rush by the river, caught up in one's thoughts, scarcely noticing the water; one pays careful attention to it, noticing its smell and appearance. If one notices trash, foam on the surface of the water, chemical smells, and the like and does not feel separate from the river but a part of it, one will feel that he himself is sick and be moved to do something about it.

A remarkable demonstration of what Nhat Hanh is talking about can be seen in John Seed. Seed is the founder and director of the Rainforest Information Centre in Australia and one of the founders of the Rainforest Action Network (RAN) in the United States. He has created projects that protect the rain forests while providing sustainable income—such as the growing and marketing of tree crops like Brazil nuts, rather than endeavors in which the trees are cut and sold for lumber—for indigenous inhabitants in South America, Asia, and the Pacific. He lectures and leads environmental workshops all over the world and has produced several videos on the rain forest and five albums of environmental songs.

Though he no longer does so, for about seven years Seed practiced intensive Buddhist meditation, which he then felt to be the foundation of his life. Entirely unexpectedly, while participating in a demonstration to save a rain forest that was located close to where he lived, he "felt the forest inside of him . . . calling to him." This sounds very much like an experience of nonseparation between himself and the world. Seed says that it was the most powerful experience of his life. It was also transformative, leading him to devote all of his energies thereafter to the protection of the rain forest. Shortly after this experience he stopped meditating. He says that now the rain forest is his spiritual practice, which he describes as an experience of no-self. Instead of doing a Buddhist meditation, he goes into the forest and surrenders himself to it; lying on the ground, he feels the sap of the tree of life running through all the trees in the forest and through himself. Lest this sound too strange, he backs his experience up rationally, pointing out that it is a fact that every breath of air that we take connects us to the atmosphere of the entire planet. For Seed this is not just something that he thinks or believes; it is something that he feels physically. Though he no longer identifies as a Buddhist and no longer does Buddhist practice, John Seed represents the epitome of the process that Thich Nhat Hanh has talked about. It is clear that it was Seed's coming to feel his inseparability from the rain forest that was the key event that compelled him to act on the rain forest's behalf.

Gary Snyder is a Pulitzer Prize–winning poet, an Ecology Hall of Fame honoree, and an Engaged Buddhist deep ecologist whose life exemplifies the manner of being under discussion here and whose poetry and prose celebrate and advocate that way of life. His book *The Practice of the Wild* is a modern classic that articulates a visionary ecological ethos in poetic prose that celebrates the "etiquette of freedom" and the "practice of the wild." Snyder's vision is equally an expression of Zen Buddhism and of deep ecology, both of which are fundamentally based in nondualism.

We need, Snyder says, to overcome the dichotomy of the civilized and the wild. We think of the wild as disorderly and threatening, but in fact it is orderly and the very foundation of life or even life itself. In fact it is very much like the Dao: beyond categories, self-organizing, playful, surprising, complete, complex, simple. In our efforts to tame the wild and to live within what we have tamed, we distort and diminish both life and ourselves. We need to realize that we ourselves are permeated by the wild in the genetic structures that we have inherited from other life forms, in the air that we share with the entire planet, in the microorganisms that make us their home. We are but a small part of the "big potlatch," the great give-and-take of the impermanence and openness that is life. We need to learn to live the "etiquette of freedom" and avoid the "stinginess of spirit" that can cause us to misbehave in the potlatch, taking too much, treating it wastefully, boasting of our power, and not giving back our share.

None of this means a "return to nature" in which human culture and civilization are negated. That would be to embrace only one side of the polarity. Human language and human cultural products are part of human nature; they are what we do naturally, says Snyder. Children learn language naturally, just by living, within a few years of birth. That is the work of nature; schools add only the thinnest veneer to what is in fact a product of the wild, outside of our control. Other species have their own ways of communicating, appropriate to their own natures, societies, and civilizations. We are not different.

We need, says Snyder, "a civilization that can live fully and creatively together with wildness." The wild is orderly; it is lawful. If we break its laws, we die. Yet it *is* wild, beyond our "control." If we learn how to stop separating ourselves from it, we will overcome the dichotomies we have created—the separation of the sacred from the physical, the human from the natural, the mind from the body. Living within the orderly wild, obeying its laws, and discovering its openness and fecundity, we may learn the nonduality of freedom and responsibility, spontaneity and discipline. Here in the practice of the wild is where Zen, with its strict monastic rule that leads to freedom, meets deep ecology.

In order to live thus, we must settle into a particular place and let it teach us. The natural is always the particular, so we must learn the contours of the land of a particular place, the names and habits of its biota, its patterns of change over time. We may learn from native peoples, who understood themselves as part of the potlatch and knew how to live intimately within the natural world. But because our species has misbehaved so grievously in the potlatch—we have overextended our numbers, taken over vast expanses of land with agriculture and cities, and exterminated many other species—we must go beyond simply living and begin seriously practicing responsible stewardship in community with other local people and with the local ecosystem.

Snyder's activism grows directly out of his personal commitments. He is best known in this respect for his work in founding and working with the Yuba Watershed Institute in the Sierra Nevada, California, where he lives. The institute works with both privately owned lands and Bureau of Land Management lands, researching and experiment-

ing with projects in order to create a model area capable of both protecting wildness and diversity and serving as a home for humans while
maintaining both ecological and economic sustainability.

Joanna Macy—who spent formative years with Buddhists in India,
Tibet, and particularly in Sri Lanka learning from and chronicling the
Sarvodaya Shramadana movement—is another important Engaged
Buddhist deep ecologist, known especially for her contributions to
nuclear guardianship and despair and empowerment work. In deep
ecological fashion, she urges us, as she states in her *World as Lover,
World as Self,* to fall in love with the world and to learn to know it as
oneself. She sees herself and each of us as not separate from the many
processes that constitute the world, but as a "flow through" of those
processes of matter, energy, and information.

Macy's nuclear guardianship work is an effort to bring responsible
attention to the problem of nuclear waste. It is based upon the Buddhist principle of mindfulness, of facing reality or recognizing what is
as what is. She sees us as a society participating in a massive denial of
the danger of what we have created in nuclear waste, a deadly hazard
to all of life for hundreds of thousands of years. Most of us literally
want it to be "buried" far away from wherever we are. She argues that
to do so is only to increase the danger because with the materials out
of sight, we will not know when containers have corroded or split or
when there has been a leak. We need to do just the opposite: watch the
materials vigilantly, generation after generation, as a spiritual responsibility to future generations. We have the technology, she argues, to
contain and monitor the materials and sites; all we need to add is our
mindful attention. She imagines Guardian Sites as places of pilgrimage, of remembrance of the past and future, and of spiritual service to
others.

Macy's despair and empowerment work developed from her own
despair at the desperate state of the natural world. When in the midst
of her ecological activism her mind was penetrated by the depth of the
illness of the natural world and the likelihood that this could culminate
in an ecological catastrophe resulting in the end of conscious life on
Earth, she entered into a profound and debilitating despair, which she
has found echoed in many people, the despair that we cannot simply

assume that we will pull through. She emerged from this despair with a method to move from despair to empowerment, a method that she shares with others in her workshops.

The first step in moving out of despair, Macy says, is to acknowledge that it is justified—the world really is in frighteningly serious trouble. It is natural to grieve over such a devastatingly vast loss. We must, she says, allow ourselves to feel these feelings. They are important because they are the key to our recognizing our connectedness with the suffering planet. The pain we feel at the hurt the world is suffering is the world's own pain, expressing itself through us, who are part of it. The pain can bring us back in touch with our connection, our participation in the world's life. We should share with others who feel similarly our concerns for the planet, our despair, hopes, and fears. This will show us that we are not alone in these feelings and give us encouragement. When we allow our feelings to be felt and shared with others, it releases energy. We are moved to respond by caring for the hurt, just as if we had injured one of our own limbs; as we respond, we leave behind the powerlessness of despair and recommit, together with others, to taking action to save the planet we all love. Macy now hopes for what she calls the "Great Turning," away from the industrial growth society, which she is certain is doomed, to a life-sustaining civilization, which she is by no means certain we will reach.

Arne Naess, John Seed, and Joanna Macy together created the idea of the Council of All Beings. This is a ritual in which humans speak for other species that cannot speak for themselves. The ritual may begin with mourning for the suffering of the planet. Participants may silently think of a particular species and spend some time contemplating it. They then gather in a circle, and each person identifies himself or herself as a particular species, a river, or any particular living thing. Each speaks spontaneously and in the first person for that particular life form, alluding to its condition, its needs, hopes, and fears. Through this ritual or playacting, other beings' experiences and needs become more real for people, and people feel more keenly their interrelatedness with other species. This ritual, like the despair and empowerment workshops, empowers people by helping them be more conscious of their connections with other species and with the planet. It ends with people recommitting themselves to the struggle on behalf of all species and life itself.

Ecology Initiatives

THAILAND'S ECOLOGY MONKS

The ecology monks of Thailand largely evolved from that country's development monks, whom we discussed in chapter 5. For the most part, their focus has been upon Thailand's widespread and rapid deforestation, a result of the government's decision in the early 1960s to promote fast economic growth. Since that time deforestation has gone forward swiftly and in a widespread manner, with devastating ecological effects. Between 1976 and 1989 the country lost 28 percent of its forest cover. The UN Environment Program states that two-thirds of Thailand's wildlife habitats have been destroyed by deforestation. In 2001, 176 people died as villages were buried by mudslides that resulted from massive flooding linked to deforestation which had made mountainsides into barren wastelands. In 1988, 317 people were killed in similar fashion. After the 1988 tragedy the government passed a ban on logging; however, a great deal of illegal logging still continues. The loss of forests also continues from slash-and-burn agricultural methods, as well as from the conversion of more and more forest land to farmland for the production of cash crops by hard-pressed villagers.

Ecology monks have taken multiple approaches in working with deforestation. Some monks advocate that rural populations responsible for tree cutting be moved away from the forests. The majority, however, practice a combination of education and ritual in order to help local people protect the forests. In many cases the people simply don't know about more eco-friendly forms of agriculture and often don't understand the relationship between their cutting of trees and the hardships they suffer from erosion, flooding, mudslides, soil degradation, and the like. The ecology monks teach them and help them to find ways of supporting themselves that do not require them to cut trees.

Like the development monks, the ecology monks perform traditional rituals with changes that give a religious meaning to their projects. They have adapted the traditional practice in which the laity gives robes and cash to the temples in order to earn merit by inviting people to give tree seedlings to the temple instead. Some of the seedlings may be planted around the temples, but the majority will be used for reforestation. Usually trees that can produce an income for villagers without being destroyed (such as fruit trees) are used for this purpose. People are very happy to participate in such a ceremony, which has the multiple benefits of carrying an aura of sanctity, earning merit, reforesting, and promising a future income for the villages.

One of the most dramatic and creative projects of the ecology monks is tree ordination. This is another adaptation of a traditional ceremony, the ordaining of a monk. Of course a tree cannot be made fully into a monk, but just as a monk is ritually made into a sacred object by his ordination—a sacred object whom it would be the very worst karma to harm—so a tree is "ordained" and made into a similarly sacred object whom it would be the very worst karma to harm. Typically trees are ordained in order to protect an entire forest in which the ordained trees are the oldest and largest. Many villagers, including the village headmen and other local dignitaries, accompany the monks to the part of the forest where the oldest trees are found. A ceremony very much like a monk's ordination is then held. The climax of the ceremony occurs when monks wrap the saffron monks' robes—themselves very much regarded as sacred objects—around the trees. Water sanctified by the monks may then be sprinkled on participants and observers, or the headmen may be invited to drink some of the water to bring home to them the seriousness of their duty to protect the forest. The senior monk then declares that the entire forest has been sanctified; not only must no trees be harmed, but within the entire forest no wildlife may be killed or harmed. Patrols may be set up to guard the forest and ensure that it remains free from harm.

Major logging, of course, is not done by local people but by large logging companies or "businessmen." Thailand's forests are home to extremely valuable species, such as teak. To stand in the way of major logging enterprises that want prizes of such high value is a perilous endeavor. Monks working to protect the forests from time to time face serious challenges and even threats. If the monks seem to become too "political," they may lose the support of the public or of powerful

Tree Ordination, Thailand. Source: Susan M. Darlington.

people. Ecology monks Phra Prajak and Ajarn Pongsak had to disrobe (give up their status as monks) when they themselves, rather than the forests they were trying to protect, became the focus of controversy and legal action. In 2005 the development/ecology monk Phra Supoj Suwajano was killed after protesting illegal logging in a forested area of 280 acres that he was trying to preserve; the acreage was desired by a local group of "businessmen."

ZEN MOUNTAIN MONASTERY

Zen Mountain Monastery and its Mountains and Rivers Order—the name comes from the "Mountains and Rivers Sutra" of Japanese Zen master Dogen—led by Zen master John Daido Loori, is the home of the Zen Environmental Studies Institute, which offers in-depth training that puts Zen students, environmental workers, legislators, and administrators in touch with nature. Sharing Gary Snyder's view, the institute emphasizes trusting the inherent intelligence of wildness, which has known how to take good care of itself since it came into being; all we have to do is not disturb it. Upon incorporation, Zen Mountain Monastery as its first order of business wrote into its bylaws that 80 percent of its 250-acre site would remain forever wild—not managed, manicured, or developed. Moreover, it holds that its sangha is constituted by all sentient and insentient beings inhabiting this land. It offers programs that aim to provide an opportunity for people to come to love nature and feel an identity with it through such immersion experiences as wilderness exploration, wilderness skills training, and backcountry wilderness retreats.

An experience of connectedness with the natural world, we are told, has spiritual benefits: it gives practitioners a sense of personal peace and contentment, a feeling of belonging that erodes feelings of aloneness and alienation. On another level, when people feel connected with the natural world, they come to care about it. Such caring, the Zen Mountain Monastery people believe, provides the most solid basis for preventing harm to nature by humankind. Zen Mountain Monastery expresses this itself with its full program, which integrates science and spirituality and engages in environmental activism, environmental

Daido Roshi on a Wilderness Trip in the Adirondack Mountains.
Source: Mountains and Rivers Order National Buddhist Archives.

monitoring, research on pollution, and the maintenance of a nature sanctuary. The related Green Dragon Society practices "advocacy for the insentient" on Zen Mountain Monastery lands. Thus is Buddhist environmental activism rooted in Buddhist spirituality.

INDIVIDUAL INITIATIVES

Many other Engaged Buddhists are doing work on behalf of other species or the planet, too many for all to be mentioned here. I will briefly mention a few Western examples to give an idea of the work that is being done.

For the last five years Jim Gollin has chaired RAN, dedicated to the protection of old-growth forests and their ecosystems. Like Roshi Bernie Glassman, Gollin unabashedly works with the capitalist world. Convinced that the major corporations have immense power—more than some nations—he finds it imperative to move them toward actions that are friendlier to the planet. While he participates in some very confrontational actions, he ultimately aims to make friends with corporation leadership. For example, to persuade Home Depot to stop selling lumber from Amazon rain forests, RAN arranged for people in 162 Home Depot stores to broadcast a message over their store intercom systems on the same day; the message announced that there was a sale on wood from the heart of the Amazon and that the taking of this wood was leading to the dislocation of indigenous communities, the degradation of the soil, and the destruction of Mother Earth. Astonishingly after such a strong action, the Home Depot leadership ultimately became part of RAN's team. Together they helped put pressure on Boise Cascade to stop cutting old-growth forests. They also persuaded Kinko's not to use paper from old-growth trees and Citigroup not to finance the destruction of old growth. Reflecting on this work, Gollin, in Buddhist fashion, rejects the idea of a struggle of good against evil, with one side out to vanquish the other. He notes that corporation heads are like everyone else and want to feel good about what they do, though he says that it is often necessary to get their attention first with strong actions.

Engaged Buddhists have also made important contributions on behalf of animals. Brad Miller, a student of San Francisco Zen Center, founded the Humane Farming Association. With 190,000 members, its aims are to protect farm animals from cruelty, to protect humans from dangerous chemicals used in farming, and to protect the environment from the harmful effects of farming. The members engage in anti-cruelty investigations and exposés, prepare national media advertising campaigns, and offer emergency care and refuge for abused farm animals. Their most successful program has been their Boycott Veal campaign, which has reduced the sales of veal by 70 percent in the United States.

Vanya Palmers, another student of the San Francisco Zen Center, has taken relatively aggressive action on behalf of factory-farmed animals in Switzerland and Austria, particularly pigs. He has lobbied, broken into locked buildings, filed charges against schools and farms, organized rallies, and staged direct actions. People have enjoyed it when he has taken piglets to schools and public places in order for people to meet and get to know them, and they have been horrified by the forty-five-second film he has created and shown in commercial theaters in which viewers see pigs living in nature and then see them locked in cages, screaming. In another action, Palmers arranged for the Swiss capital of Bern to be showered with feathers from old pillows to draw attention to the plight of factory-farmed chickens, who live their entire lives in tiny wire cages without even enough room to turn around, a practice subsequently outlawed in Switzerland.

CHAPTER 7

Human Rights and Criminal Justice

The Buddha did not speak of either human rights or criminal justice. In response to current social needs, Engaged Buddhist leaders are creating new forms of Buddhist discourse and practice in these areas. While these are based upon traditional Buddhist values and ideas, they entail entirely new applications of them.

Human Rights

The subject of human rights in Buddhism has occasioned more debate than any other aspect of Engaged Buddhism. Some scholars, both Asian and Western, argue that the concept of human rights is a Western concept that has no place in Buddhism. Others, Asian and Western, argue that the concept of human rights, while Western in origin, has its equivalent in Buddhism. Both sides have their supporting arguments. The bottom line, though, is that many Asian Engaged Buddhist activists readily use the concept of human rights in their work. In some instances—notably the Burmese, Tibetan, and Cambodian—human rights form the very foundation of the cases that activists make on behalf of the people they represent.

The case against human rights in Buddhism, made by some scholars but not by activists, is in brief as follows. The concept of human rights appears to be based upon individualism—that is, an emphasis upon the individual at the expense of the group, a value characteristic of Western, but not Asian, societies and one apparently irreconcilable with Buddhist ideas of no-self and interdependence. After all, if there is no self, who would be the owner of any rights? Human rights recognize property rights, which might be seen as strengthening the ego and its grasping. Human rights seem to give greater value to the human being than to other sentient beings, whereas in Buddhism humans are simply part of the class of sentient beings. Human rights emphasize rights, whereas Buddhism emphasizes responsibilities. Finally, the idea of human rights takes an adversarial stance with respect to conflict, whereas, as we have seen, Buddhism takes a nonadversarial approach and Asian societies prefer the idea of harmony.

Regarding the concern that the concept of human rights is incompatible with the Buddhist philosophy of no-self, we can state very simply that this is a red herring. Buddhist ethics function quite well without a substantial self. For example, the first lay precept invites one to abstain from taking life. Who is it that takes this precept? Who abstains from taking life? Whose life is protected? The answer to any of these questions cannot refer to a substantive being possessed of a self, and yet the precepts function quite adequately to guide morality. The same is true for human rights. Both precepts and rights require only a functional person, not an ultimately real human self.

Regarding the right to property, we must bear in mind that the recognition of this right is not a license to amass and hoard vast riches to the detriment of others, nor is it a justification for consumerism. As we have seen, those concerns are addressed by other Buddhist teachings. The human right to property is the right not to have one's property seized by another. It is based upon the recognition that humans are embodied and therefore have physical needs. Some states, among them China and Burma, violate this right by seizing monasteries (in Tibet), homes, and means of livelihood. The concern for the right to property is active among Engaged Buddhists at this level; it can be a matter of life and death. Such issues as the grasping behavior of the ego and the imbalance of wealth between the global North and South are genuine concerns among the Engaged Buddhists, but they are addressed by means other than the denial of a right to property.

The case for the fundamental compatibility of human rights and Buddhism is made in a variety of ways. Several scholars recognize a link between the Five Lay Precepts and some of the rights in the United Nations' Universal Declaration of Human Rights (UDHR); for example, the first lay precept, which emphasizes our responsibility not to kill, implies a right to life; your duty implies my right. Similarly the second lay precept, which emphasizes the responsibility not to steal from others, implies a right not to be stolen from—that is, it implies a right to property.

Another approach to making a Buddhist case for human rights involves the Buddhist emphasis upon the innate human capacity for enlightenment and the preciousness of the human birth as the only form of life that can realize Buddhahood. This view of humankind justifies giving precedence in human rights to human beings. Some scholars also find support for human rights in the Buddhist emphasis on nonviolence and compassion. Through these teachings and values Buddhism expresses how precious each and every human life is, logically implying that we should take good care of and nurture each human life and certainly avoid inflicting harm upon them. Aung San Suu Kyi is among those who express this view, scorning the Burmese military regime's pretence that human rights are out of keeping with the humane values of Buddhism. Other Buddhist teachings and practices, as we have seen, ensure that this limited precedence given to humans is not extended to the point of justifying harm to nonhuman species or the environment. One also finds ample support in Buddhist scriptures for the idea of human equality, a concept vital to human rights.

Those who have given the subject the most thought recognize that a free and open society is essential to the central Buddhist project of self-development toward Buddhahood. For these Buddhist intellectuals, our most essential human right goes beyond those listed by the United Nations: we have a natural right as human beings to self-development toward Buddhahood. This right requires a very free society in which there is freedom of conscience and religion, freedom of speech and association, an open sharing of ideas, and so forth—all important human rights protected by the United Nations.

On the basis of such considerations, most of the philosophical concerns about human rights vis-à-vis Buddhism can be answered. One issue that remains difficult to resolve and continues to be debated is whether the adversarial nature of human rights is compatible with Buddhist nonadversariality and preference for harmony. Beyond these philosophical considerations, however, the most important point—

and a point beyond debate—is that Asian Engaged Buddhist activists do use human rights language in making their cases to a global audience. It is important to note that they do not as readily embrace all Western political concepts; very few of them, for example, use justice language to make their case, perhaps seeing it as too apt to serve as a rationale for revenge. They have no philosophical problems in embracing the idea of human rights, though. Indeed they have little patience with the autocratic governments that would deny them these rights and see the philosophical arguments against human rights as smoke screens used by tyrants to conceal the unjustifiability of their abuse of power.

In the case of Tibet, for example, since the Chinese took political control of Tibet in 1959, the Tibetans have suffered greatly under Chinese rule. As noted in chapter 4, an estimated one million people, about one-sixth of the population, have died as a result of the Chinese occupation, either directly—from reprisals, executions, torture, and harsh conditions in prisons and labor camps—or indirectly—from famine induced by Chinese agricultural policies. The International Commission of Jurists concluded in 1959 and 1960 that there was a prima facie case of genocide against China in Tibet. Since part of traditional Tibetan Buddhism includes revering the Dalai Lama as head of the state, loyalty to the Dalai Lama—that is, traditional Tibetan Buddhism itself—is threatening to Chinese claims of sovereignty in Tibet. Because of this, Buddhism itself has been systematically targeted in Tibet, with over six thousand Buddhist monasteries and temples destroyed, many monks and nuns forcibly defrocked, and many others imprisoned for demanding the "right" to practice their religion freely. At present, 79 percent of Tibetan political prisoners are monks or nuns. Female political prisoners die at a rate of one out of every twenty-two. Many monks and nuns suffer forced "reeducation" or indoctrination. All of these are human rights abuses. Other human rights frequently ignored by the Chinese in Tibet include those of freedom of speech, freedom of the press, freedom of assembly and movement, and the right to peaceful protest. Tibetans wanting to flee the country must do so in secret. The eleventh Panchen Lama, a figure close to the Dalai Lama in traditional Tibet, has been held incommunicado for years. The most pernicious of China's actions is the relocation of large numbers of ethnic Han Chinese people into Tibet, together with "reduced child quotas" for many Tibetans, making the Tibetans a minority in their own country. It is a practice called "cultural genocide" that threatens their future existence as a people.

To all of China's actions the Tibetan leadership has responded with principled nonviolence and a global campaign for the respect of human rights in Tibet. It should be clear why the Tibetans have made human rights the cornerstone of their campaign for independence or self-determination. The Chinese are guilty of what global standards recognize as gross and systematic violation of the Tibetan people's human rights, to the extent that their existence as a people is threatened and their present way of life has been severely constrained and distorted. Chinese violation of the human rights of the Tibetan people is the core language that the Tibetans use as they make their appeal to the global community for redress of their situation—in formal petitions, speeches, books, and Web sites. (Try typing "Tibet" and "human rights" into an Internet search engine and you'll see.) They consistently defend the idea and importance of all the human rights specified in the UDHR, arguing that these rights must trump objections by nations such as China, which claim that outside powers should not interfere in their internal concerns. For an economically, politically, and militarily weak country like Tibet, appeals on the basis of human rights are one of the few forms of power for which they can reach—that and the appeal of the moral high ground that they occupy in their struggle with China.

Another Buddhist country that emphasizes the idea of human rights is Cambodia. Cambodia suffered the Khmer Rouge auto-genocide, in which between one million to over two million people (out of a population of seven million) were killed. In order to recover from the chaos—and the corruption, lawlessness, and climate of impunity that has followed—the leaders of the Cambodian Buddhist Sangha decided that the people needed instruction in fundamental moral principles—specifically the Five Lay Precepts and human rights. Today Buddhist monks in Cambodia are taught basic information on international human rights as part of their training, with the expectation that they will include instruction in human rights in their regular sermons. They are taught to see the common moral ground found in human rights and the Buddhist Five Lay Precepts. Thus the monks' routine teaching of morality is based upon respecting human rights and observing the Five Lay Precepts, two things that they present as virtually the same. A recent survey demonstrated that Cambodians overwhelmingly believed that the return and resurgence of Buddhism in Cambodia was the single most important cultural factor in promoting human rights in that country. Other studies have shown that, for Cambodians, to promote human rights is simply to promote morality.

Human rights are at the forefront of the struggle in Burma as well. Burma/Myanmar has been ruled since the 1960s by an autocratic military government. (The country called Burma by most of the world was renamed Myanmar by its present military rulers; one sees both names used today.) In 1988 the streets of Rangoon were filled with tens of thousands of students and Buddhist monks demanding democracy and human rights. People sang, "I am not among the rice-eating robots. . . . Everyone but everyone should be entitled to human rights." Thousands of people were killed by the government in a crackdown on the protests. Aung San Suu Kyi, who has expressly declared her belief in Engaged Buddhism, is head of the National League for Democracy, which represents the Burmese people's demands for democracy and human rights. Suu Kyi and her party won a landslide electoral victory in 1990. The military government cancelled the results and placed Suu Kyi under house arrest, where she has remained for over twelve of the past eighteen years, often without visitors for years at a time. She is far from alone; over twelve hundred people were political prisoners before the latest crackdown; no one knows how many thousands may be prisoners at the time of this writing. Aung San Suu Kyi won the Nobel Peace Prize in 1991.

What are the human rights issues in Burma? According to Human Rights Watch, systemic human rights violations in Burma include summary executions; the killing of civilians by the military; extensive forced labor and forced portage; widespread predation of the military upon civilian populations; condoned military rape of women and children; destruction of the villages of ethnic minorities; the creation of over five hundred thousand internally displaced civilians; the extensive forcible recruitment of children into the military; and restrictions on movement, assembly, and speech. The army is also known to force civilian porters to walk ahead of army units to test for land mines.

The response of Aung San Suu Kyi and the National League of Democracy has been to maintain a strictly nonviolent stance, call for a dialogue with the military rulers, and insist upon human rights. Suu Kyi emphatically rejects the government's contention that human rights are an un-Burmese, Western artifact alien to the country's cultural traditions; she points out ironically that in Asia only autocratic rulers claim that human rights violate Asian cultural traditions; the people, she says, find them entirely compatible with their values. She specifically states that human rights are compatible with Buddhism because of the great value that Buddhism places on the precious human birth and the great human capacity to attain enlightenment.

Burma was back in the news in 2007 as a result of dramatic street protests led by Buddhist monks. Much of the world had forgotten that monks had done the same thing in 1988 and was puzzled by the sight of Buddhist monks leading street protests, but this was nothing new for Burma. The 2007 demonstrations began as protests against the high fuel costs that resulted when the military regime lifted price controls. The Burmese people, who had been subjected to steady impoverishment under the military regime, felt that these high fuel costs were ruinous. The demonstrations for this reason quickly became, once again, demonstrations against the military regime and for democracy and human rights.

Why did *monks* (and nuns) prominently take to the streets—twice now—on behalf of democracy and human rights? It is not difficult to understand that their most fundamental motivation is compassion for the suffering of the people. As we saw in chapter 2, the first premise of Buddhism is that suffering, both mundane and spiritual, is a problem that should be eliminated, and Buddhism is conceived as a set of methods and tools to do so. Therefore, when Buddhists see profound suffering, it is natural for them to consider how to eliminate it. The question then becomes how one can best help. As in the Sarvodaya movement, so also in Burma the characteristic Buddhist thinking is

Burmese Monks Protesting against the Government, 2007.
Source: Democratic Voice of Burma.

present: if there is a problem, the proper course is to identify its cause and then remove it. In Burma the military regime is the cause of the suffering; if it is removed, the suffering should stop.

Certainly the involvement of the highly revered monks in the street protests was an excellent strategic move. In many respects, the monks represent the conscience of the nation. If the monks say something is wrong, it *is* wrong in the minds of any Burmese with traditional values. Some monks publicly overturned the bowls in which they accept food donations, stating that they would not accept food donations from members of the regime or their supporters. This gesture was a public declaration of the moral bankruptcy of the regime. It also closed the door to the primary traditional method for earning good karma for any regime member or supporter who might be worried about all the bad karma his actions have earned him.

Moreover, the monks are regarded as sacred in their persons; they are so sacred that the very robes they wear are sacred. Monks in the streets publicly calling for an end to the military dictatorship presented a profound dilemma to the regime. On the one hand, they could not be tolerated. On the other, to violently remove the sacred monks from the streets would be so egregious in the eyes of faithful Buddhists that it could push many fence-sitters over the edge into active opposition of the regime. The monks knew very well that they were risking their lives when they went out into the streets, but they also knew the power of their action. They were willing to sacrifice themselves for the sake of others in order to create this power.

Despite the military crackdown on the demonstrations in Burma, hope remains at this writing. Burmese activists, including many monks, have been training in strategic nonviolence for decades. Nonviolent struggle organizer Gene Sharp wrote his famous booklet, *From Dictatorship to Democracy*, to aid the pro-democracy forces in Burma, at their invitation; the booklet provides concrete methods for nonviolently working to overthrow a dictatorship. In addition to the edition in the original Burmese, the book has now been translated into the Burmese minority languages of Karen, Mon, Jingphan, and Chin (as well as Tibetan). Sharp has worked with the Burmese pro-democracy forces (and the Tibetan liberation movement), giving intensive workshops, advice, and support in strategizing. There are many more strategies available to nonviolent activists than street protests, and we may see some of these in the future.

A final form of Engaged Buddhist human rights work that we may consider is the dalit Buddhist movement. Dalits are members of the Indian social class formerly called "untouchables." For millennia they were considered to be spiritually and socially inferior—literally polluting to others—and were severely oppressed. Though discrimination against untouchables is outlawed in modern India, old attitudes die hard, especially in the villages. The former untouchables now call themselves dalit, the oppressed, as many upper-caste Hindus still despise them, requiring them to get their water from separate wells and to work in only the most menial occupations. Some Indians actively try to prevent ex-untouchables from breaking out of their oppression, and violence may flare when the dalits stand up for themselves.

When the great untouchable leader B. R. Ambedkar declared in 1935 that because of Hinduism's legitimation of the caste system, though born a Hindu, he would not die a Hindu, he set out on a meticulous search to find a religion to which to convert, not only for himself, but also for the millions of untouchables whom he believed would follow him. After an extended search, he chose Buddhism. Buddhism, he felt, was best because it also was an Indian religion and therefore not culturally alien; it was rational and pragmatic and avoided dogmatism; most important, it rejected the Hindu institution of caste and taught human equality.

Some scholars claim that the Buddha did not actually reject the caste system per se but simply stepped outside of it when he stepped outside all of society's nets upon leaving home to become a wandering seeker. This view overlooks the Buddha's pointed critique of caste in the *Vāseṭṭha Sutta* of the *Majjhima Nikāya*. There the Buddha is recorded as saying that unlike the differences between the classes of birds, fish, quadrupeds, and snakes, whose differences are real and innate (that is, based upon birth), the class distinctions among humans—specifically the four *varna,* the great classes (commonly called castes) of Hindu society—are based upon occupation and are not real but merely conventional, assigned by society. It is statements like this that drew Ambedkar to Buddhism.

The practices of the Buddha as a teacher confirm this passage affirming intrinsic human equality. The Buddha accepted men and women into the community of monks and nuns regardless of their caste or class status, gender, or former occupations. Persons of both genders and all classes were recognized by the Buddha during his lifetime as having attained enlightenment. Everyone was given the teachings "with an open hand"—that is, the Buddha did not hold back teachings from some people depending upon caste, as some Hindu teachers did. Everyone had an equal opportunity to practice and was invited to listen, learn, and undertake the effort to see what he or she could achieve.

When Ambedkar publicly converted to Buddhism in 1956 by taking the Three Refuges (in Buddha, Dharma, and Sangha) and the Five Lay Precepts, approximately 380,000 other ex-untouchables converted as well. There are about eight million Buddhists in India today, the vast majority of them ex-untouchable "new Buddhists." They believe that with their conversion they are reborn. This belief is the key to the psychology of the movement: the former untouchable, despised by the Hindu caste system, is no more; a new person, intrinsically equal to everyone else, is born.

Though conversion is an act of defiance, a repudiation of the converts' old lives and the society that created them, life conditions do not change automatically with conversion. Some dalits' lives have improved over the past few decades due to government programs promoting education for dalits and setting aside jobs for them. The lives of others have scarcely changed at all. They may live in the most appalling conditions. They may need homes that keep out the elements, adequate nutritious food, access to clean water, and health care. They may need literacy, education, training in a skill to earn a living, or access to work that is not degrading. While such material improvements are necessary, a change in their psychological state is also essential. The conditioning to which untouchables have been subject produces mental states of hopelessness and helplessness because in the past nothing they did could make a difference in their lives. Under such conditions, people give up. Buddhism's strong suit, in comparison to many other approaches that might be taken to fixing the untouchables' problems, is mental discipline, the intentional replacement of unwholesome and unskillful states—such as hopelessness, defeatism, self-loathing, anxiety, and depression—with wholesome and skillful states, such as effort, determination, inner peace, and clarity. With a new attitude, it may be possible for the former untouchables to do something about their material needs; without it, it is not possible. For this reason the study and practice of the Dharma, which might seem like a low priority given their other needs, is an acute need for the new Buddhists.

It must be said that the dalit new Buddhists have received only a small fraction of the support that they have needed from other, established Buddhists. At least one group has energetically stepped forward, however: the Friends of the Western Buddhist Order (FWBO), based in the United Kingdom. In 1979 the leader of the FWBO, the British-born monk Venerable Sangharakshita, founded Trailokya Bauddha Mahasangha Sahayaka Gana (TBMSG) as an Indian branch of the FWBO. There was originally considerable British leadership in the TBMSG, but now the leadership is almost entirely Indian. The FWBO continues to engage in substantial fund-raising for TBMSG.

TBMSG does its best to teach the Dharma to the new Buddhists, organizing lecture tours, publishing educational materials at low cost, and offering Dharma and meditation classes and retreats. All of these activities are very well received, but they are able to reach only a fraction of the millions of new Buddhists, many of whom would very much like to know more about their new religion. Similarly the social welfare branch of TBMSG, Bahujan Hitay (named after the Buddha's encouragement to his disciples to go out into the world "for the welfare of the many"), offers multiple programs and services, but these again can meet only a fraction of the need. The programs include kindergartens, residential school hostels, after-school programs, literacy classes, vocational classes, health care services, nutrition supplement programs, small business start-up assistance, and sports and cultural activities. All of these programs are run by the Indian new Buddhists themselves.

There continue to be mass conversions from among the ex-untouchable dalits (conversion to Christianity and Islam is also popular), despite the fact that conversion has become a hot political issue in India. Recently the government passed laws making mass conversions more difficult (at least one of these has been overturned by the Indian supreme court) and sometimes may prohibit them or turn people away from them. On the other hand, Hindu nationalists sometimes regard Buddhism as a part of Hinduism and as a consequence do not object to conversions to Buddhism to the degree to which they may object to conversions to Christianity. Of course Buddhists—especially the dalit new Buddhists—reject this pernicious form of inclusivism, which attempts to erase Buddhism's distinctiveness by claiming it as no more than a sect of Hinduism. In fact it is in this respect that the dalit Buddhist movement is unique among Engaged Buddhist movements: only the dalits are helping to reestablish Buddhism in the land of its birth, where it has been absent since some time after the twelfth century.

Criminal Justice

If a society that claims to be just is to engage in the practice of imprisoning people, that practice must be justified—that is, the justice of the practice must be demonstrated persuasively. From a Buddhist point of view, the imprisonment of wrongdoers can be understood as an opportunity for the working out of the negative karma generated by harmful actions, but there are other ways for that karma to be worked out, so imprisonment is not *required* by karma. Imprisonment can be justified in order to protect innocent people and also to protect those who might harm them (protecting the latter from doing themselves karmic harm by preventing them from taking harmful actions that would result in negative karma). However, imprisonment cannot be justified as retribution, which is seen in Buddhism as no more than revenge or retaliation—that is, an expression of anger—and is therefore unacceptable. In the end, only the protection of society and the criminal are viable justifications for imprisonment from a Buddhist perspective.

Furthermore, as we saw in chapter 2, there is more to a prisoner than the crime he committed. Therefore, those who have committed crimes cannot be simply written off as evil and put out of the sight of humanity in prisons to be forgotten. It follows that conditions and programs in prisons must provide genuine opportunities for the reform and rehabilitation of the prisoners. Conditions in many prisons today are hardly conducive to the reform of the inmates, to say the least. On the contrary, they can be violent, overcrowded, and degrading and often tend more to strengthen tendencies toward criminal behavior rather than reform. Introducing opportunities for Buddhist practice into prisons is one small way of making prison institutions more conducive to the reform of prisoners.

All the major Western and some Asian Buddhist traditions are involved in teaching prisoners to meditate. While it faces some special challenges, teaching meditation in prisons is not fundamentally different from teaching meditation to anyone else. In and of itself teaching meditation in prisons seems to be a borderline or overlap area between traditional and Engaged Buddhism. Thus we see people who are primarily meditation teachers, such as S. N. Goenka of India and Zen master John Daido Loori of Zen Mountain Monastery in New York, heavily invested in this kind of prison ministry. However, socially engaged aspects of this work seem to naturally and inevitably evolve once a group is working with prisoners.

In order to be admitted to teach in the prisons and in order for prisoners to be allotted time, space, and materials for meditation, a number of meditation teachers and prisoners have had to be involved in lawsuits forcing the prisons to open to Buddhist ministry alongside the already established Christian, Muslim, and other ministries. It was through this kind of litigation that Zen Mountain Monastery's extensive prison ministry program began. After the litigation was successful, the abbot of Zen Mountain Monastery, John Daido Loori, founded the National Buddhist Prison Sangha (NBPS) in 1984. The program has grown to become one of the major Buddhist prison ministry programs in the country. It offers meditation instruction, spiritual guidance, and practical support to male and female prisoners in all types of prisons. It is open to all kinds of Buddhists, as well as to those who do not identify as Buddhists but who want to study meditation. The training program goes well beyond meditation to include instruction in ethics, health, art, work attitudes, and social interactions. Much of the instruction is by correspondence; the NBPS currently handles over one thousand inmate letters each year. In addition, the NBPS is heavily involved in conflict resolution and human rights advocacy within the criminal justice system. It works to end capital punishment, change the violent nature of the prison system, and eliminate discrimination, especially discrimination against the practice of Buddhism within the prisons. The program has been very successful, with reports that inmates make noticeable improvements in the following: developing awareness of habitual unwholesome behaviors; taking responsibility for past and present actions in regard to both themselves and others; maintaining sobriety; avoiding destructive behaviors and reincarceration; and making constructive contributions to society. One of the most telling outcomes of the program is that the inmates themselves have started a number of victim awareness groups that promote empathy for and outreach to the victims of their crimes. Through the sale of their artwork inmates have also raised money for juvenile delinquency prevention programs.

Another innovative program is evolving at Zen Mountain Monastery. Upon their release, two former inmates who had practiced meditation in the NBPS prison program came to live at the monastery for a year. At present, others are considering doing the same. To move from a prison into a monastery makes intuitive sense. Prisoners often have trouble moving directly from the total absence of freedom in a prison to the complete freedom on the outside; a monastery environment—especially one in a remote location—keeps one away from many temptations and provides a very structured living situation with clear rules, guidance, and supervision. It provides a positive environment where one's personal growth is a major objective and there is considerable camaraderie for support and uplift. While this will never be an appropriate kind of program for more than a few, for those prepared for and interested in such a living situation, it makes a natural kind of halfway house and a positive step for former inmates to move their lives forward.

Shugen Sensei (left) *and Prison Inmates at Green Haven Correctional Facility. Source: Mountains and Rivers Order National Buddhist Archives.*

Another very large program of teaching Buddhist meditation in prisons is seen in the work of S. N. Goenka. The film *Doing Time, Doing Vipassana* documents the remarkable success that Goenka has had working in Tihar Prison, India's largest prison and widely regarded as one of the harshest in the world. The (non-Buddhist) inspector general of the prisons, Kiran Bedi, as part of her overall effort to change Tihar Prison from a place of misery into a place for personal development, was looking for a way to give prisoners the skills they needed to handle themselves better. Upon the recommendation of one of the guards, who himself practiced vipassana (insight meditation), Bedi invited Goenka to lead one of his ten-day meditation trainings in the prison. Goenka was willing but said that some guards had to be trained first since if the guards still treated the prisoners with harshness and cruelty, it would not be possible for the prisoners to change. Bedi sent some of the most aggressive guards to take the program and observed that they seemed calmer upon their return. She decided to let the program proceed.

In the first ten-day program over one hundred prisoners and jail staff took the course together, side by side. Goenka and his wife lived in the prison for all ten days. They began by requiring everyone to take the Five Lay Precepts for the duration of the course. They then proceeded with breath meditation and insight meditation. The program seemed successful, and five more courses were taught. The results were so positive that Bedi asked Goenka to teach the course to one thousand inmates at once. The outcome was very positive. Prisoners reported that their feelings of anger and thoughts of revenge were weakened and receded. Many admitted to themselves for the first time that they had done something wrong, and they regretted it. Many wept. They began to see how their minds worked and to recognize their habitual thoughts and patterns of reaction. They began to realize that they had control over these things and that they could change. Some even said that it had been worth coming to prison just to learn these things. Prison officials point out that it is impossible to help people if they don't want to help themselves. It was vipassana that was able to get the prisoners to the point where they want to help themselves. Ultimately Tihar Prison established a permanent vipassana center offering courses twice a month; prisoners from other prisons can come to study vipassana, and Tihar inmates who have taken the course serve as volunteers, helping and preparing food. People outside the prison saw changes in former inmates' behavior when they were released. Recidivism declined. The government of India decided to encourage the study of vipassana in all the prisons in the country.

Preliminary results of studies in India and the United States show a reduced recidivism rate among former inmates who have taken vipassana courses while in prison. Other studies show decreased substance abuse, decreased psychiatric symptoms, greater self-control, and greater optimism. Further studies, many funded by the National Institutes of Health, are under way in the United States. If vipassana is demonstrated to significantly help former prisoners such that they do not commit new crimes and have to return to prison, it will be a significant contribution not only to the life of the individual prisoners, but to society as well.

In addition to the meditation programs, some people involved in prison ministry find other elements of Buddhist teachings particularly helpful for prisoners. In Buddhism there is a famous story of a criminal named Angulimala that has become an inspiration to prison inmates and those working to support them. During the time of the Buddha, Angulimala was a bandit and serial killer who cut off the fingers of those he murdered and wore them on a cord around his neck like a necklace. After a prolonged reign of terror, he one day encountered the Buddha on the road. Intent on making the Buddha his next victim, Angulimala stalked the Buddha but somehow could not catch up with him. As the Buddha walked away from him, Angulimala called to him, "Stop, monk, stop!" The Buddha replied, "I have stopped, Angulimala; you stop too." Something in the Buddha's words and bearing got through to Angulimala, who did stop. He threw away his weapons, became a bhikkhu, and lived harmlessly for the rest of his days. When those whom he had previously terrified threw stones and broken pottery at him, he bore the attacks quietly.

Stories of transformation like Angulimala's and teachings like the idea of Buddha nature mean a great deal to prisoners involved in Buddhist practice. Such stories and teachings do several things at once.

First, they look unflinchingly at the reality of violence—the violence of the prisoners' past actions as well as the violence of the prison realm in which they currently live. This is often part of the process through which the prisoners come to accept responsibility for what they have done. Anthony Stultz, a Buddhist minister and psychotherapist who is active in prison ministry, combines the Angulimala story with a chanted moral precept: "We take complete responsibility for our own life and all of our actions." At the same time, the Angulimala story clearly expresses the hope that even the most depraved can change. Thus the liturgy continues, "We affirm our own being and acknowledge it as a path to awakening and freedom." Stultz emphasizes how important the Buddha nature teaching is to inmates, who, he says, feel that they are morally defective. The Buddha nature teaching assures them that we are born with "Original Blessing, not Original Sin," as Stultz puts it. We are not inherently depraved or morally defective. We were born with human decency, and we can regain that decency. Importantly, the determination to transform oneself is made on the basis of an inner morality rather than an imposed outer morality based upon obedience to an external authority. It is an inner decision made on the basis of seeing clearly what one is, has been, and can be. In sum, transformation is grounded in facing one's own reality; accepting full responsibility for one's actions; and affirming that inner transformation is possible, for one's own sake and for that of others. This, as Stultz rightly points out, is something that is distinctively Buddhist in the Buddhist approach to prison ministry.

Another aspect of Engaged Buddhist work in the area of criminal justice is help for the professionals that work within the system. We have seen that Goenka requires prison guards and officials to take vipassana courses either prior to or along with prison inmates. He does this so that at least some professionals in the prison system will understand the vipassana program and therefore be able to help integrate it and its practitioners into the larger prison system. Of course taking the vipassana course changes the prison staff just as it changes the prisoners, giving them more self-knowledge and self-control and less reactivity and anger. Such changes, in turn, inevitably transform the prison environment.

Another example, on a much smaller scale, of work to transform professionals within the criminal justice system can be seen in a retreat that Thich Nhat Hanh held for police officers in Madison, Wisconsin. This retreat came at the request of Cheri Maples, a police captain who enjoyed Thich Nhat Hanh's retreats but wondered if what she had learned there could be reconciled with her responsibilities as a police officer: she carried a gun and knew that she might have to use it, whereas Thich Nhat Hanh asks his students to take the Five Lay Precepts (in his revised version, the Five Mindfulness Trainings), the first of which states that we should not kill. When Maples asked about this potential conflict, she was told that she should think of herself as a fierce bodhisattva, a being whose entire motivation is the welfare of others but who knows that sometimes fierceness is the most helpful way to serve others. She was told that she could carry a gun as long as she did so with mindfulness and with the motivation of compassion—who else, they said, would they want to carry a gun but someone with compassion and mindfulness?

Because of the pressures of their job, police officers often develop a painful state of mind that is hyper-vigilant, tense, aggressive, and defensive. This state of mind develops gradually, but many find that they are unable to put it down when the work shift is over. In the Wisconsin retreat Nhat Hanh taught them practices to relax their minds, cultivate compassion, and interact with each other without aggression. Maples reports that as a result of such practices over time, she felt her heart softening, even on the job. She tells the tale of answering a domestic violence call one night: a man who was separated from his wife was refusing to give their child back to the mother after the child's visit with him, in effect holding the child hostage. The mother and child were both very frightened. Maples convinced the man to let the child go, and then instead of immediately arresting him as she ordinarily would have done, she sat down and talked with him. Within five minutes he was crying, and pain that had been expressed earlier as anger came out. Three days later the man saw Maples off duty on the street, came up and hugged her, and told her that she had saved his life that night. Maples considers her ability to work with this man in this way as the fruit of her mindfulness practice.

We have seen that Buddhism does not allow us to dismiss any prison inmates as beyond the pale, too far gone. Even for those who have committed the most heinous crimes, Buddhism offers hope and insists that we give them the opportunity to change. Some prisoners admit that they need the structure and limits of prison in order to avoid reoffending. But even if they remain in prison for the rest of their lives, if they make an effort and if conditions in prison support them in their efforts, they may make some progress for their own sake (not only in this life, but in future lives as well, from a Buddhist perspective) and perhaps become capable of offering something of value to others. It certainly happens.

Fleet Maull is one example of an inmate who practiced Buddhism, changed, and became a person who could give something of value to others. Imprisoned for fourteen years for drug smuggling, Maull took novice monastic vows in prison to help support a profound change of heart. He founded not only the Prison Dharma Network, a support group for Buddhist prisoners and prison volunteers, but also the National Prison Hospice Association, a program for visiting with dying prisoners. Maull's original hospice program in his own prison became the prototype for the national program, which assists in the formation of hospices in other prisons. Having served his time, he now publishes, leads retreats and workshops, and works for peace. Another example of a prisoner whose life has become a major asset to others is Jarvis Jay Masters, a San Quentin death row inmate. Masters wrote a powerful book, *Finding Freedom: Writings from Death Row,* which paints a stark and intensely real portrait of life in a Level 4 (out of four felony levels) prison and documents his transformation into a compassionate peacemaker within the prison with the help of his Tibetan Buddhist practice. This book is widely read and has changed many lives. One never knows who might be capable of such change and such contributions.

Capital punishment of course is the ultimate dismissal of the human value of the one who is executed. Engaged Buddhists are unanimously opposed to capital punishment. Buddhist laywoman Melody Ermachild Chavis has shed a great deal of light on the subject in reflecting on her work as a mitigation lawyer for felons facing a possible death sentence. A mitigation lawyer looks into a client's background to see if there are circumstances that would help a jury understand why he or she may have committed the crime of which he or she is accused and perhaps to have mercy on her client, declining to sentence him or her to death. Mitigation has no bearing on the question of guilt, only on the matter of punishment.

Chavis writes, "Many death penalty proponents believe that evil infects people like my clients, who must therefore be extinguished." In the context of courtroom decisions, this belief is a matter of life and death. As a Buddhist, Chavis believes instead in the ideas we saw in chapter 2: because there is no fixed soul in a human being, a person cannot "be" evil in an absolute or final way. People are unfolding processes. In twenty years of mitigation work Chavis has come to be a strong believer in karma because she has found again and again a great web of karmic causality in the lives of her clients. Take the case of Ben, for example. Ben was in prison for shooting and killing a policeman. Without in any way minimizing the gravity of that act and bearing in mind the preciousness of the lost life and the grief the loss caused many others, even going into her research overwhelmed by Ben's guilt, Chavis found the following: Ben was conceived in Jonestown, Guyana, just before the mass suicide of 909 people there in 1978. Ben's mother, who was a member of the cult, survived and came back to America. Practically everyone she knew was dead and she had very few resources, so Ben and his mother spent a lot of time in homeless shelters; she was alcoholic and suffering from post-traumatic distress syndrome. He was raised in a ghetto neighborhood, surrounded by gangs and guns, becoming an alcoholic himself. Ben's is a unique case, but Chavis finds that poverty, violence, abuse, and trauma are constant factors in the childhoods of all of her clients. Many have neurological damage.

We know enough sociology by now to know where a situation such as Ben's is likely to lead. Indeed sociology confirms the Buddha's teaching on causation: when this is, that is; this arising, that arises. Events occur in response to the causes and conditioning of preceding events. Chavis says, "For twenty years I have searched for evil, and nowhere have I found it. I find causes and conditions aplenty." The Dalai Lama agrees. He writes of our innate "need for others' kindness, which runs like a thread throughout our whole life. It is most apparent when we are young and when we are old. But we have only to fall ill to be reminded of how important it is to be loved and cared about even during our prime years. Though it may seem a virtue to be able to do without affection, in reality a life lacking this precious ingredient must be a miserable one. It is surely not a coincidence that the lives of most criminals turn out to have been lonely and lacking in love."

This being the case—and it is—Engaged Buddhist activists ask: How can we execute? How can we respond to a person who has been cruelly formed in a life without love, and who has acted violently out of that loveless life, and execute him? This is not to say that Ben is blameless. He did make choices. But given the causal conditions that shaped those choices, how can we execute? Execution can be justified only if one is convinced that the person being executed "is," in his very being, evil and that transformation in that person is impossible. Chavis writes, "I really believe in transformation, because I've seen, so many times, people avowing their karma. That's our chant, that's our vow, and it happens. We realize what we've done, we really get it, and we begin to transform it." It will be no surprise to learn that Chavis and many other Engaged Buddhists stand in meditative vigil at every state execution and work hard to end the death penalty.

CHAPTER 8

Challenging Tradition

Prompted by compassion and by belief in the preciousness of a human birth, work to promote human well-being is prominent among the Engaged Buddhists, Asian and Western. However, this work is dogged at times by traditional thinking about karma and gender.

Trouble with Karma

We have seen that karma is a crucial element in traditional Buddhist thought; without it traditional Buddhism is inconceivable. It continues to play an essential role in the thinking and action of Engaged Buddhists today, as we have also seen. However, a number of Engaged Buddhists have significant complaints about the idea of karma or at least about the way that karma is traditionally understood. Some of them have proposed alternative ways of thinking about karma that may avoid some of the problems of traditional Buddhist thought on the subject. What kinds of complaints do the Engaged Buddhists voice about karma?

One kind of concern has to do with the traditional teaching that some of the most significant events of one's current life are the result of one's actions in past lives. While the Buddha decidedly did *not* teach that everything that happens to a person in his or her life is the karmic outcome of that person's deeds in previous lifetimes, the Buddha *is* recorded as having said that the particular circumstances of one's birth—one's gender, health, wealth, physical looks, etc.—are the karmic consequences of actions in past lives. The view, then, is that one earned the particulars of one's birth. If one is born into an impoverished family or with a disabled body, this is not just bad luck but

a caused and appropriate outcome. This view causes Engaged Buddhism, and modern Buddhism in general, quite a few difficulties.

One example can be seen in the work of Dr. B. R. Ambedkar, the
former leader of the dalit, "oppressed" Buddhists, the members of the
formerly untouchable class in India who convert to Buddhism as a
vehicle for escape from oppression. Ambedkar's primary enemy was
the Hindu caste system. A secondary enemy, however, was one that
Buddhism shared with Hinduism: the concept of karma. Understandably Ambedkar rejected the idea that the particulars of one's birth—
including the caste and economic status of one's family—were caused
by one's previous deeds—that is, one's karmic inheritance—as this
teaching seems to imply that people born as untouchables earned that
status by misdeeds in a previous life and in that sense their low birth
was apparently justified. Ambedkar, who earned numerous advanced
degrees in the West, was aware that this idea was entirely at logger-
heads with the socio-scientific idea that socioeconomic classes are simply social constructs and that it is no more than a misfortune, with no
moral desert implied, to be born into a low socioeconomic class. Social
science implies that one who is born into poverty and low social class is
a victim, one who got an unfairly handicapped start in the race of life.
Karma, in effect, blames the one born into poverty for his own plight.
The two views could not be more opposite.

Ambedkar was well aware that in order for the untouchable class to
raise themselves to a higher standing in the world, they would need to
be free of self-hatred and self-blame, free of thoughts that they deserved
their misfortune; and instead confident in the belief that they deserved
better. This seemed impossible if traditional teachings on karma were
maintained. As a consequence, Ambedkar dropped discussion of these
aspects of karma from his representation of Buddhism to the untouchables. These could not be the Buddha's teachings, he felt, as they were
out of line with the general thrust of the Buddha's message, which
was to give hope to humankind for self-improvement. Teachings on
karma and caste were the very beliefs in Hinduism against which he
was struggling. They must therefore be later interpolations into the
Buddhist texts. When Ambedkar wrote *The Buddha and His Dhamma*,
his distillation of the Buddha's teachings, he emphasized instead the

facts that the historical Buddha repudiated the Hindu caste system, accepted disciples of all social classes, and treated them entirely as equals, socially and spiritually, within the Buddhist community.

Textual considerations are not our concern in this book, but we should note that Ambedkar's "solution" was one of the more problematic attempts by an Engaged Buddhist to resolve a genuine dilemma in the traditional teachings. Ambedkar redefined the cause of suffering, or *duḥkha* (the Second Noble Truth), as external social factors such as poverty, rather than as the usual internal psycho-spiritual causes, craving and ignorance. While this "solution" avoided the problem of blaming the victims of poverty for their own suffering, as traditional Buddhism could be accused of doing (that is, implying that the poor have only themselves to blame for their poverty), it was at the cost of weakening the traditional strength of Buddhism, its insight into the psycho-spiritual nature of the human condition and the psycho-spiritual dynamics of the way in which we create our own experience.

A second way in which karma is a problem for the Engaged Buddhists is with traditional interpretations that karma implies passivity. Aung San Suu Kyi, the leader of the democracy struggle in Burma / Myanmar, states that one of the greatest difficulties her movement faces is that the Burmese people typically think that karma means fate—that is, their suffering at the hands of a brutal military dictatorship is the result of their past actions, so there is nothing they can do but bear it until that karma has been exhausted, at which point their suffering will end of itself. Unlike Ambedkar, who veers away from the teachings of the Buddha as recorded in the scriptures, Aung San Suu Kyi and many other Engaged Buddhists remain on solid scriptural ground when they argue that the understanding of karma as passivity is contrary to the teachings of the Buddha. The Buddha emphasized many times that any teaching that makes people believe that there is no point in making an effort to engage in spiritual practice is contrary to his teachings and indeed a pernicious teaching that no one should accept. He taught, in fact, in order to encourage people to make an effort. He discouraged people from wondering about their karmic inheritance, saying that it was so unknowable that it would make their heads split if they worried about it excessively! Karma only takes us to the present moment; at this moment, we must make an effort, creating new causes and conditions that will shape our experience in the future.

It is an uphill struggle in many Asian and even Western contexts to convince Buddhists that karma does not mean passivity, even though the Buddha clearly rejected this understanding and strongly emphasized the importance of making an effort. Aung San Suu Kyi struggles to convey to traditionally minded Burmese that karma means action and is therefore the opposite of passivity, but she seems to make little progress in convincing such people to change their understanding of an idea so deeply entrenched in the culture. Just as the attainment of Ambedkar's goals requires a change in thinking about karma, so too in Suu Kyi's case a change in thinking about karma is a necessity for sufficiently large numbers of Burmese to actively engage in the struggle for democracy.

The status of women in Buddhist countries is affected by both kinds of difficulties with karma. Ouyporn Khuankaew, a Thai laywoman, heads the International Women's Partnership for Peace and Justice, which works to end violence against women and to build women's leadership. In Thailand prostitution and the sex trade are huge problems. Some extremely poor rural families sell their daughters into prostitution in order to bring some cash into the home. The girls suffer conflicting emotions: shame at what they have become, a sense of karmic fatality that such is the fate of women with women's poor karma (if they had better karma, they wouldn't have been born as women!), and a sense that in this way at least they are repaying their parents' care for them, paying them back in the only way possible for a woman. Karma therefore justifies to these girls what has happened to them and instills in them a passive, fatalistic attitude toward it.

Ouyporn challenges this idea of karma. In a form similar to Ambedkar's, Ouyporn states in her organization's brochure that the suffering women face is not a product of individual karma, action, or misfortune but is a result of societal structures and is a form of violence against women. She believes that once women recognize that their suffering is not their fault, they will realize that they can end it. Once they are able to move beyond blaming themselves, they will be empowered to identify violence as violence, understand its root causes, look for solutions, and work for change. Ouyporn draws upon both Buddhist teachings and feminism for her ideas. When I once asked her if there was anything in Buddhism that she would challenge, she replied that there were two such things. First, she criticizes the popular understanding of karma as fate, with its resultant passivity. Second, she criticizes the idea that being born a woman is the result of bad karma. Her response to these ideas is that whatever you are doing *now* is what makes you who you are. Karma is action, she says, and it is important to focus on the present.

Rethinking is also going on in Engaged Buddhist circles, as well as contemporary Buddhist practice circles, with respect to karma and disability issues. As we have seen, the Buddha did state that the conditions of one's birth, including the relative beauty and soundness of one's body, are the karmic fruit of one's past deeds. In Buddhist countries people traditionally saw the presence of disabilities as evidence of bad karma from former lives. Though Buddhist teachers have emphasized that disability should call forth our compassion and our readiness to help, popular understanding based on the idea of karma has provided a rationalization for people to turn their backs on the disabled; it thus has been a psychological barrier against assisting the disabled or improving their condition. This interpretation of karma has been so common that modern reformers in countries like Japan bitterly blame Buddhism for much of the super-added suffering of disabled people beyond the physical suffering directly caused by their disabilities—their rejection by society, their treatment as pariahs, and the lack of interest in helping them.

Oddly enough, given this legacy, in the modern West some disabled people have found Buddhism to be a significant help, especially in coming to psychological terms with their disability. Frequently they cite the following as helpful: Buddhism makes suffering and dealing with suffering its central focus rather than sugarcoating it; Buddhism differentiates pain (as in the unavoidable physical pain that may be the direct result of a disability) from suffering (the psychological reaction to one's circumstances) and gives concrete methods for eliminating the suffering—for example, how to handle the mental pain of facing a disability and craving a cure; Buddhism shows that our ideas of "normalcy" are constructed by society and provides tools for deconstructing such ideas when they are internalized; Buddhism puts the final responsibility for dealing with one's circumstances into one's own hands rather than into those of God, gods, or fate, an attitude that the disabled find empowering; perhaps most important, Buddhism gives people tools to deal with their anger, fear, and despair and the clinging and craving that often arise in painful ways.

With regard to the question of karma, some disabled people simply ignore traditional teachings, finding them irrelevant, as did Ambedkar. Others accept the idea that something they did in a past life caused them to be born disabled, but they do not think of that as a punishment, or a negative thing, simply a fact. They may feel that if they made some bad choices and acted in harmful ways in a past life, in this life they have the opportunity to do better. The fact that the Buddha himself discouraged people from pondering their past lives is known in the community of disabled people working with Buddhism, validating the decision of many to simply focus on this life and handle it well.

These two troublesome issues concerning karma—its interpretation as blaming the victim and as implying passivity—are both difficult and important, not only for Engaged Buddhism but also for contemporary Buddhism in general, and require extensive discussion by both scholars and practitioners. Many Buddhists feel that even if a society accepts the idea that birth into unfortunate circumstances is a consequence of actions in past lives, the proper response by Buddhists should not be to blame or reject those born into poverty, disability and the like. The past life is gone; the person who did those supposed bad deeds is no more. It is wrong to dwell upon what came before, not letting the person who is before us now move on but seeing him through the eyes of the past. In the present, the proper response should be compassion, support, and/or helpfulness, as appropriate. As for the passivity that many Buddhists have taken from the teaching of karma, it is simply a misunderstanding of the Buddha's teachings. The problem is that this misunderstanding is widespread and deeply entrenched in many Buddhists' minds. The only remedy for this problem is education.

To raise questions makes it possible to start finding answers. As we have seen, Engaged Buddhists have creative interpretations of karma. Susan Moon, the editor of *Turning Wheel*, makes explicit that the positive view of karma implied by some of the Engaged Buddhists discussed above is one conducive to social engagement. "I love karma," she has written, "and here's why. . . . It's never too late [and] everything I do matters." When urging people to take action, Engaged Buddhists focus on the present and future aspects of karma: one is constructing the future with what one is doing now. Clearly this is empowering; it is the very opposite, in fact, of what Engaged Buddhists say have been earlier *mis*interpretations of karma, which have emphasized what one had done *in the past*. Since there is nothing one can do about the past, such interpretations were *dis*empowering and created a sense of resigned fatalism in many people (against which Aung San Suu Kyi struggles to this day in Burma). But if one emphasizes the idea that what one does now determines the future—as is also inherent in the idea of karma—then people feel that the future is open and what they do makes a difference. Such an emphasis changes everything as far as engaging one's life is concerned, be it spiritually or socially. The Engaged Buddhists are on very strong ground in arguing for this slight shift in perspective. After all, *the Buddha taught*. If the Buddha had believed that everything was somehow fated from our past actions, what would have been the point of teaching? He taught in order to encourage us *to take action, to do something* about our situation. In fact the Buddha argued strenuously against fatalism, condemning it as the view with the most pernicious spiritual consequences.

This nonfatalistic, activist view of karma can be embraced even by Buddhists who hold to the traditional Buddhist worldview emphasizing the transience of all things. While that worldview might make it seem as if all effort to improve things in the world is futile, Melody Ermachild Chavis, who works against the death penalty, draws the opposite conclusion. "As Buddhists," she writes, "we know that the death penalty and prisons and everything else we see will pass away some day. Things arise and things dissolve and karma is created and burned up again. But meanwhile, what do we do? I believe that in order to transform our own karma, we work for a more just society." The idea is this: we are alive, here and now. To choose passivity, to choose not to act, is a form of action; it is to construct a future on the basis of passivity, to allow what has come to us from the past to continue, becoming seemingly more inevitable with every day that passes. Alternatively we can focus on the present and by our actions in the present add a new bit of reality that, when added to what has come to us from the past, transforms the present reality to one degree or another.

Gender Issues

The legacy of Buddhism for women is mixed. On the one hand, it is greatly significant for women that the Buddha specifically stated that women have the same spiritual potential as men. In recognition of this potential, he established the order of bhikkhunis (nuns) for women. This became not only a vehicle for committed Buddhist practice for women but also a respectable alternative to marriage for women in a society in which the only other alternatives were to work as servants or prostitutes. Women flourished for centuries within the bhikkhuni order, their accomplishments acknowledged by the Buddha and remembered in the remarkable book of *Therigāthā* poems. On the other hand, as institutional Buddhism evolved, it developed characteristics that were less supportive of women. Bhikkhunis were governed by the "eight weighty rules" *(gurudharma)*, attributed to the Buddha, which systematically placed the bhikkhuni order in a subordinate position to the order of bhikkhus. Within the Buddhist monastic order, seniority is determined by how long a person has been a monk or a nun. The eight weighty rules render the entire bhikkhuni order junior to the entire bhikkhu order, thus requiring even a most senior nun to rise respectfully and venerate even a most junior monk. The rules require a transgressing bhikkhuni to be disciplined by both the bhikkhuni and bhikkhu orders, while the same is not required of the bhikkhus. Similarly bhikkhunis must pass the rainy season retreat where there are bhikkhus in residence, while the reverse is not true. The bhikkhus are to admonish the bhikkhunis, while the reverse is not true. Finally, a female novice must be ordained by both the bhikkhuni and the bhikkhu orders, while the same is not true of a male novice.

These rules were probably instigated to protect the Buddhist order at a time when society demanded greater controls over women.

As Buddhism became more institutionalized over time and the wandering orders of bhikkhus and bhikkhunis evolved into settled monastic orders, the effect of these rules was to subordinate the entire bhikkhuni order to the entire bhikkhu order both administratively and in terms of education and training. As a consequence of the latter, the bhikkhunis' accomplishments declined. The bhikkhunis had an additional handicap. Traditional views of karma (among both Hindus and Buddhists) were popularly understood to mean that since birth as a woman was clearly less desirable (as experienced in that time and place) than birth as a man, women in general had inferior karmic legacies as compared to men. This view would have combined well with the visible subordination of the bhikkhunis to the bhikkhus in the eyes of the laypeople. In addition, it was believed that the more exalted the one to whom one gave a gift, the more merit one earned by one's donation. Since the bhikkhu order was plainly more exalted than the bhikkhuni order—both in traditional beliefs about karma and in institutional fact—the giver who wanted to earn the most merit possible from his or her gift would clearly prefer to give to the bhikkhus. The Buddhist monastic orders in India relied upon popular support in the form of food and other donations. Scholar Nancy Falk reasons that the bhikkhunis' inferior level of accomplishment and status in the Sangha, plus traditional views of women's karma, were responsible for drastically declining material support for the bhikkhuni order in India, gradually resulting in fewer, hungrier, and more destitute bhikkhunis, as reported by pilgrims to India from China, who said that the bhikkhunis were much poorer than the relatively comfortable bhikkhus with whom they were contemporaries. Falk surmises that this situation was responsible for the demise of the bhikkhuni order in India centuries before the bhikkhu order ended there. Ultimately the bhikkhuni order died out altogether in the Theravada sect throughout the Buddhist world. A variety of quasi-nun arrangements developed, differing from country to country, as women took varying numbers of vows. These women have the status of neither a bhikkhuni nor a laywoman.

In the Mahayana world the bhikkhuni order lived on. However, as a general rule, the nuns received less support than the male monks. To give just one example, in 1913 the Soto sect of Zen in Japan spent 600 yen per year for each bhikkhuni for education, training, and upkeep, while it spent 180,000 yen per year for each monk. This kind of radical inequality was typical throughout the Buddhist world. As nuns and quasi-nuns from throughout the Buddhist world began to meet in the twentieth century to consider their status, the following picture emerged as the rule: the nuns' education and training was inadequate for them to practice the Dharma effectively. This was virtually a universal concern among the women. Their other major interest was the possibility of reviving the bhikkhuni order within the Theravada sect. Engaged Buddhist leaders are part of the advocacy for its revival.

Why is there any question at all about reviving the Theravada bhikkhuni order if there are women who want to be bhikkhunis? The issue is that, as we have mentioned, the eight weighty rules require a woman who wishes to become a bhikkhuni to be ordained by both the bhikkhu and the bhikkhuni orders. Since the bhikkhuni order has died out, there are no existing bhikkhunis to participate, as required, in the ordination of new bhikkhunis. Therefore, according to conservative members of the Sangha, it is impossible to ordain new bhikkhunis at all. This argument is unconvincing to those who wish to reinstitute the order; they say that one could simply use Theravada bhikkhus and Mahayana bhikkhunis to ordain new Theravada bhikkhunis, especially since the Theravada Vinaya (monastic rule) and the Mahayana Vinaya are the same. This argument does not satisfy the conservatives, who insist upon Theravada bhikkhus and Theravada bhikkhunis to ordain Theravada bhikkhunis.

There are several reasons why many Buddhists wish to see the bhikkhuni order revived in the Theravada world. Probably the first in most people's minds is to make the practice of the Dharma fully available to women, as the Buddha intended. This author once heard Thich Nhat Hanh begin a public speech by addressing the Theravada bhikkhus, who were seated in the front row. He said that by allowing the bhikkhuni order to die out, they had not taken good care of what the Buddha had given them. This was a powerful argument for a conservative order, the Theravada, which prides itself in handing down Buddhism as the Buddha taught it.

More subtle reasons for reviving the bhikkhuni order have to do with its effect on the status of women. Sexual slavery and prostitution are huge problems in Thailand. Ouyporn Khuankaew, in addressing this issue, points out the indirect role played by Buddhist monastic institutions in this problem. There is a connection, she says, between the bhikkhuni issue and prostitution. Of the three hundred thousand bhikkhus in Thailand, 80 percent are from very poor families. The monasteries have become respectable places where poor young men can in effect get a job (as bhikkhus), bringing respect to their families. The sons of those families also come from small towns and rural areas to city monasteries in order to get a (secular) education, availing themselves of the time-honored institution of serving as "temple boys," who do menial jobs for the monks in the monastery and in return receive room and board in the monastery and the oversight of the monks while they complete their education. In effect, this is an economic safety net system that Thai society has evolved for men and boys. Since the bhikkhuni order scarcely exists, there is no comparable economic safety net or educational support system for girls and young women. This is one of many reasons why the bhikkhuni issue is very important. If poor women could be educated for free in a safe and respectable place like men, they would become financial assets rather than burdens to their families. If they could earn merit for their families by becoming bhikkhunis, they would also have greater value in their families' eyes. Either or both of these possibilities could substantially reduce the practice of selling girls into sexual slavery.

In fact the bhikkhuni order is being revived in the Theravada world. This process began in 1988, when five Sri Lankan quasi-nuns received bhikkhuni ordination in a Taiwanese (Mahayana) temple in Los Angeles, but upon return to Sri Lanka they found no supporting structure and failed to establish a permanent foothold for bhikkhunis. In 1996 ten Sri Lankan quasi-nuns were ordained in Korea, but there only the bhikkhus participated in the ordination ceremony, and without bhikkhuni participation, the ceremony did not meet Sri Lankan standards.

Finally, in 1998 thirty Sri Lankan quasi-nuns received bhikkhuni ordination with the participation of Sri Lankan (Theravada) bhikkhus and Taiwanese (Mahayana) bhikkhunis. This ordination was well received because the Chinese bhikkhuni order was originally established by Sri Lankan monastics. Thus it is not difficult to see the continuity between the original Sri Lankan bhikkhuni order and the newly reestablished one. There are now over five hundred Theravada bhikkhunis in Sri Lanka, far more than the quota of five required for ordaining other bhikkhunis into the Theravada order.

Thailand is a Theravada Buddhist country where the bhikkhuni order was never established, even in the old days. In 1928 a law was passed making it illegal for a Thai bhikkhu to ordain a woman, even as a novice (the "lesser" ordination, to precede full ordination by two years), much less as a bhikkhuni. Today, however, the bhikkhuni order is being introduced by the former Buddhist scholar Dr. Chatsumarn Kabilsingh, who was ordained in Sri Lanka in 2003 as the first Thai Theravada bhikkhuni ever, Venerable Dhammananda. She carefully chose to be ordained by bhikkhus belonging to a Theravada subsect, the Siam Nikaya, which came to Sri Lanka from Thailand, as well as the Sri Lankan bhikkhunis. Thus she too can point to the continuity in her monastic lineage between the order that she is establishing in Thailand for women and an order that existed in Thailand centuries ago. Today there are approximately sixteen women novices and six bhikkhunis in Thailand.

The illegality of ordaining women in Thailand demonstrates how conservative Thailand's monastic establishment is. Ven. Dhammananda has had to put up with considerable harassment and threats since her ordination, but she persists. What is her motivation? First is the wish to give something back to Buddhism. The Buddha established four legs to the Sangha: bhikkhus, bhikkhunis, laymen, and laywomen. Without all four legs, she argues, Buddhism is weakened. In many ways Dhammananda has been preparing for this role all her life. Her mother ordained as a Mahayana bhikkhuni and established a popular and well-supported temple (even now not officially recognized by the government as a Buddhist temple) outside Bangkok, where Ven. Dhammananda was raised. She grew up learning the liturgy and practices. She became a well-known and prolific Buddhist scholar and did exhaustive research on the history of the bhikkhuni order. When her mother became too old and ill to give Dharma talks and officiate at ceremonies, she took over, even while still a laywoman.

Second, Ven. Dhammananda wants to make bhikkhuni practice available to women. Before Dhammananda ordained, the only way for a woman to practice Buddhism in Thailand other than as a lay-woman was as a *mae ji*, the Thai form of quasi-nun. The *mae ji*, however, are not a respected institution. They are generally regarded by the public either as heartbroken women whose love lives have failed or as impoverished beggars, not as women with religious vocations. They are poorly educated and are often barely tolerated in the monasteries as cooks and domestic servants for the bhikkhus. However, when the Buddha instituted the bhikkhuni order, he specified that the bhikkhuni would not cook, sew, or act as servants to the bhikkhus; he protected their religious vocation. These rights have been lost to women lacking the protection of the bhikkhuni status.

Third, Ven. Dhammananda wants to make social services available to women that the bhikkhus cannot provide. Long before her ordination, she established the Home of Peace and Love at her family temple as a place for unwed mothers, a shelter for any woman who needed one, or simply a site for poor women or girls to get access to education and support. Dhammananda is well aware from her discussions with women who come to her that there are many things that the women simply cannot talk about with the bhikkhus, such as their husbands' abusive behavior or any emotional issues, yet for which they need counseling and practical support. She believes that only a healthy bhikkhuni order can help women with such needs.

Yet another reason for establishing the bhikkhuni order in Thailand concerns gender equality and respect. In Thailand one sees many gestures of respect, particularly bowing with the palms held together; the lower one bows, the more one conveys one's own humility and the exalted status of the other. One bows particularly low before the bhikkhus, often with knees, and even hands, on the ground. Even the Thai king bows before the monks. When there are only male bhikkhus, one realizes after a while that one is living in a place in which men and

women regularly bow deeply before some men, but no men ever bow
that deeply before any women. This is powerful body language; though
it is not so intended, it is a constant reinforcement of popular notions
of the socially and karmically inferior status of women. With ordained
bhikkhunis, one returns to a society in which men and women bow
deeply before some men and some women, the bhikkhus and the
bhikkhunis. It becomes clear that what is being honored is the religious vocation, and any gender implications are erased. This author
witnessed members of the local community bowing deeply with clear
devotion to Ven. Dhammananda as she walked in her neighborhood
on her regular early morning rounds, accepting the food gifts of devout
laypersons, male and female. It was a moving, disorienting, and reori-
enting sight.

At Dhammananda's temple, enshrined upon the altar, next to the
Buddha, is a large and beautiful statue of the first bhikkhuni, Maha

A Woman Bows before Ven. Dhammananda on Her Alms Round.
Source: Sallie B. King.

Pajapati, seated in the lotus posture. At the daily and weekly services the community hears chanted the names of "our female Buddhist ancestors," the earliest community of bhikkhunis. On the grounds, one sees a beautiful and moving statue of a bhikkhuni in service to her community, with children surrounding her. With these reminders of the important women in Buddhism's past and the promise of bhik-khunis in Buddhism's future, it is a different world than the one that one encounters at any other temple in Thailand.

Another remarkable Thai Buddhist woman and Engaged Bud-dhist leader is the laywoman Ouyporn Khuankaew, mentioned above, founder of the International Women's Partnership for Peace and Jus-tice. With her partners, Ouyporn, as she is known, leads workshops and trainings for women in such subjects as Buddhist peacemaking, active nonviolent resistance, and leadership for social change. Their work combines feminism, social activism, and Buddhist spiritual prac-tice. One of their central emphases is the empowerment of women. They work with refugee women, women activists, and women who have suffered abuse; women come from Thailand, Cambodia, Burma, Tibet in exile, and Ladakh to participate.

One example of Ouyporn's work is her innovative approach to working with women who have suffered rape, beatings, and abuse. As in many patriarchal countries, women in Thailand who suffer such attacks experience an additional level of suffering owing to the mes-sages that they have internalized from their society, religion, and cul-ture. In the Thai case this means that women frequently feel a great deal of guilt at having been raped or beaten, whether by strangers, hus-bands, or boyfriends; they may believe it was their fault that they were attacked, that they deserved the abuse they have suffered because of their actions in past lives or this life—in other words, they brought it on themselves. Ouyporn directly criticizes such a belief and the tra-ditional notions of karma that are behind it, emphasizing that karma doesn't mean a focus on the past; it means action, and action means change now. She teaches about structural violence, patriarchy, and a financial system that leaves women dependent upon men. Women leave Ouyporn's workshops empowered, going home to tell their friends, "It's not your fault when your husband beats you!" They are empowered by understanding, but also by gaining inner peace and strength through mindfulness meditation, yoga, community building, and the nonhierarchical, participatory nature of the learning. This kind of teaching has never been offered by the bhikkhus. It comes from Ouyporn's combination of feminism and Buddhism.

Buddhist women in the West have worked on different kinds of issues. The contributions of Buddhist feminist scholars such as Rita Gross, Anne Klein, Diana Paul, and Susan Murcott, as well as Thai scholar Chatsumarn Kabilsingh, have been very important in rediscovering the history of women in Buddhism. Their studies have made Buddhist women's stories available, analyzed patriarchal elements in Buddhism, and proposed feminist versions of Buddhism. These studies have informed and inspired work for change in individual Buddhist lives and in Buddhist institutions throughout the Buddhist world; they have certainly helped Buddhist women in Asia facing an entrenched and pervasive Buddhist patriarchal system.

Also very important has been the work of Buddhist feminist practitioners and activists, such as Sandy Boucher, Deborah Hopkinson, and Lenore Friedman. They and others have changed the face of Buddhism in the West by bringing up sensitive subjects, looking at them unflinchingly, and advocating for change. One such subject has to do with the male teacher. Originally, when Buddhism started coming to the West, the teachers were all male since that was what Asia produced. This raised questions for Westerners, accustomed to a culture in which male supremacy was no longer an unchallenged norm. In the 1970s and '80s a number of scandals erupted in American Zen and Tibetan practice centers involving (male) head teachers who made sexual advances or had sexual relations with female students. For some time, these incidents were kept buried, but eventually feminist Buddhist students insisted upon bringing them to light. Once the shock was past, the disclosures opened far-reaching discussions on many things, from the nature of enlightenment and the nature of Buddhist morality to the hierarchical nature of Buddhism, the unquestioned trust in the teacher, the structure of power in Buddhist practice institutions, and the pattern of male supremacy. Two major outcomes resulted. First, the American Buddhist teachers' association agreed upon moral guidelines prohibiting sexual relations between teacher and student. Second, many major Buddhist institutions reorganized their power structure and decision-making processes, removing power over non-spiritual matters from the head teacher and either investing it in a board or opting for collective decision-making processes.

Not as a result of these scandals but as an inevitable product of the time and culture and their own dedication and work, important female teachers soon began to emerge in the West in significant numbers. This is the ultimate resolution of the problem of the male teacher.

CHAPTER 9

Conclusion

Let us conclude this volume by briefly reviewing what is *Buddhist* about Engaged Buddhism. In other words, Engaged Buddhism is a form of spiritual social activism, but what makes it *Buddhist* social activism? This is important to note not because being Buddhist makes these ideas and approaches to social activism better or worse than the Western counterparts, but only because they are different from them. Because they are different, when we encounter them, they may stimulate our own thinking in creative directions. Let us consider them in this light.

1. The signature contribution of Engaged Buddhism to global thinking about spiritual social activism is the idea expressed so well by Thich Nhat Hanh as "being peace": the idea that in order to make peace, the peacemaker needs to be peace. The peacemaker should intentionally and in sustained fashion cultivate inner peace and then go about making peace in a peaceful manner—without anger or antagonism, seeking only the good of all. Here Engaged Buddhism challenges us to consider whether "righteous" anger is ever necessary or desirable when engaging a conflict situation, as we often assume.

2. The Buddhist idea of no-self is absolutely fundamental to Buddhism and also very challenging, both philosophically and spiritually. It turns out to have profound consequences for Buddhist engagement with the world's problems. The nonexistence of an individual human self, together with the idea of interdependence, leads to the understanding that there is no absolute separation between "self" and "other"; thus "I" am not fundamentally separate from "you." As wisdom develops, one will become more and more aware of this nonseparation. This in turn has many implications.

First, since we humans are not ultimately separate, our interests co-inhere; therefore, one's thinking and acting should be nonadversarial and, again, mindful of always seeking the good of all. Second, in social work and other areas, awareness of our nonseparation from others invites us to rethink the terms of interpersonal exchanges, including such questions as "who" is giving and "who" receiving, and it helps to free us of unhelpful, egotistical attitudes. Third, in work with environmental issues, this awareness leads straight to a deep ecology perspective in which one's thinking and acting comes from an experiential sense of one's nonseparation from, one's continuity with, the world.

All these points encourage those of us raised in Western culture to consider to what extent we are, or are not, separate from other people and from our world and to be aware of the profound practical consequences of our views. They challenge us to become more aware of our interconnections and to act on that awareness.

3. Engaged Buddhist ethics, and ideally its activism, are free of judgmentalism and exhibit a radical acceptance of all persons, no matter what they may have done. Wisdom again plays a key role in developing an understanding of the way in which causes and conditions act in karmic fashion to construct the reality we encounter. Awareness of the causes and conditions that operate in people's lives undercuts the tendency to judge them harshly, while compassionate awareness of suffering maintains moral standards. The radical acceptance of all persons that results helps to steer one away from actions motivated by reactivity against someone who has done something harmful. Such reactivity is based in distaste and disapproval of the other and in feelings of one's own righteousness and superiority, attitudes that are not helpful to the situation and are themselves morally and spiritually harmful. A nonjudgmental attitude has been very helpful in work with convicts and suggests a different way of approaching criminal justice issues.

We in the Western world are deeply challenged by Buddhist nonjudgmentalism to rethink our automatic pairing of morality and judgmentalism and to consider whether we might wish to unlink these two. We also are challenged to take a hard look at our criminal justice system and consider how such a radically different way of thinking might lead us to make adjustments in it.

4. Engaged Buddhists do not think in terms of political justice, an alien concept that does not occur in Buddhism. Rather than seeing a given action as "unjust," they instead tend to see it as an unskillful response to a situation produced by karmic causes and conditions. Rather than looking for a "just" outcome, which may in their view have overtones of revenge, they look for the reconciliation of alienated groups and an end of suffering.

This approach challenges those of us shaped by Western culture to examine our thinking about justice and experiment with thinking through conflict situations without reference to ideas of justice. How would this change things? Are there any situations in which one must have the idea of political justice in order to analyze those situations properly and do what needs to be done?

5. The Engaged Buddhists deeply believe in nonviolence and are pushing the envelope to see how far nonviolence can be taken in conflict situations. In some very grave conflict situations indeed (contemporary Tibet and Burma, wartime Vietnam) the Engaged Buddhists have waged heroic, actively engaged nonviolence. Their example is inspirational. They challenge us to give nonviolence a chance.

Notes

Chapter 2: Philosophy and Ethics

P. 14. "When this exists . . .": This formula appears in several places in the Buddha's teachings. See *The Middle Length Discourses of the Buddha: A New Translation of the Majjhima Nikāya* 115.11. Translated by Bhikkhu Ñāṇamoli; translation edited and revised by Bhikkhu Bodhi (Boston: Wisdom Publications, 1995).

P. 26. Thich Nhat Hanh and the five lay precepts: Thich Nhat Hanh's restatement of the five lay precepts as the five mindfulness trainings can be found at the Web site devoted to his teachings, www.plumvillage.org/DharmaDoors/MindfulnessTraining.

P. 27. "Please Call Me by My True Names": Thich Nhat Hanh's poem and the other quotations from him in this chapter can be found in his *Being Peace,* ed. Arnold Kotler (Berkeley, CA: Parallax Press, 1987), pp. 62–69.

P. 31. Dalai Lama quote: Dalai Lama, *Ethics for the New Millennium* (New York: Riverhead Books, 1999), p. 47.

P. 32. Aung San Suu Kyi quote: Aung San Suu Kyi, *The Voice of Hope: Conversations with Alan Clements* (London and New York: Penguin Books, 1997), p. 121.

P. 32. Jiko Linda Cutts: See her "Practicing the Eight Awarenesses with a Peace Community in Colombia," *Turning Wheel,* Fall 2005, p. 16.

P. 34. Poetry teacher in San Quentin: See Judith Tannenbaum, "Human Beings Together," *Turning Wheel,* Summer 2002, p. 26.

P. 35. Gay Buddhists: See Roger Corless, "Gay Buddhist Fellowship," in *Engaged Buddhism in the West,* ed. Christopher S. Queen (Boston: Wisdom Publications, 2000), p. 271.

P. 36. Chatsumarn Kabilsingh and Geshe Sopa: Quotations are taken from notes taken by the author during the Peace Council's visit to Jerusalem, May 2–4, 2000.

Chapter 3: Spirituality

P. 40.   Fire Sermon: The Fire Sermon *(Ādittapariyāya Sutta)* can be
          found in Bhikkhu Bodhi, trans., *The Connected Discourses of the
          Buddha: A New Translation of the Saṃyutta Nikāya* (Somerville,
          MA: Wisdom Publications, 2000), p. 1143.

P. 41.   *Foundations of Mindfulness Sutta:* This work *(Satipaṭṭhāna
          Sutta)* can be found in Bhikkhu Ñāṇamoli and Bhikhhu Bodhi,
          The Middle Length Discourses of the Buddha, pp. 145–155.

P. 44.   Buddhadasa Bhikkhu: The quotation and Buddhadasa's views
          on *dukkha* can be found in Buddhadasa Bhikkhu, *Heartwood
          of the Bodhi Tree: The Buddha's Teaching on Voidness,* ed. Santi-
          karo Bhikkhu (Boston: Wisdom Publications, 1994), p. 17.

P. 51.   Richard Davidson: Research reported in *Time* magazine,
          January 19, 2007. It is available online at http://www.time.com/
          time/magazine/article/0,9171,1580438,00.html.

P. 51.   Bernie Glassman: For Glassman's work, see his *Bearing Witness:
          A Zen Master's Lessons in Making Peace* (New York: Bell Tower,
          1998), pp. 3–37 and 69, and Bernard Glassman and Rick Fields,
          *Instructions to the Cook: A Zen Master's Lessons in Living a Life
          That Matters* (New York: Bell Tower, 1996), pp. 89–91.

P. 55.   Venerable Cheng Yen: The quotation is from Yu-ing Ching,
          Master of Love and Mercy: Cheng Yen (Nevada City, CA: Blue
          Dolphin, 1995), p. 6.

P. 60.   Thich Nhat Hanh: For the precepts of Thich Nhat Hanh's Tiep
          Hien order, see his *Being Peace,* pp. 89–102, and for the story of
          the brother and sister, p. 14.

Chapter 4: War and Peace

P. 68.   *Dhammapada:* Translation adapted from Walpola Rahula,
          What the Buddha Taught, 2d ed. (New York: Grove Press, 1974),
          pp. 125, 126.

P. 71.   The Dalai Lama on empathy and compassion: See his *Ethics for
          the New Millennium* pp. 63–77.

P. 72.   Dalai Lama on the enemy: See his *Worlds in Harmony* (Berkeley,
          CA: Parallax Press, 1992), pp. 131–139.

P. 73.   Five-Point Peace Plan: See *Tibet Briefing* (New York: Office of Tibet, 1991), pp. 10–11.

P. 77.   Thich Nhat Hanh meditation on war: See *The Miracle of Mindfulness: A Manual on Meditation,* rev. ed. (Boston: Beacon Press, 1975, 1976, 1987), pp. 95–96.

P. 78.   Thich Nhat Hanh on self-immolation: See his *Love in Action: Writings on Nonviolent Social Change* (Berkeley, CA: Parallax Press, 1993), pp. 43–45. For his comment on the success of the nonviolent struggle, see p. 47.

P. 81.   Thich Nhat Hanh work with Vietnam war veterans: See the film *Peace Is Every Step.*

P. 84.   Sarvodaya peace work: For the latest information, see www.sarvodaya.org and www.sarvodayaUSA.org.

Chapter 5: Economics

P. 99.   Sutta on the "wheel-turning monarch": The "*Cakkavatti-Sīhanāda Sutta:* The Lion's Roar on the Turning of the Wheel" can be found in Maurice Walshe, trans., *The Long Discourses of the Buddha: A Translation of the Dīgha Nikāya* (Boston: Wisdom Publications, 1987, 1995), pp. 395–405.

P. 99.   Economic principles in the teachings of the Buddha: See P. A. Payutto, *Buddhist Economics: A Middle Way for the Marketplace* (Bangkok: Buddhadhamma Foundation, 1994).

P. 102.   Consumerism: I draw particularly on Stephanie Kaza, "Overcoming the Grip of Consumerism," in Sivaraksa, *Socially Engaged Buddhism for the New Millennium,* pp. 54–75.

P. 104.   Thich Nhat Hanh: On his rethinking of the precepts, see Thich Nhat Hanh, *For a Future to Be Possible: Commentaries on the Five Wonderful Precepts* (Berkeley, CA: Parallax Press, 1993).

P. 105.   For the account of the Sarvodaya movement I drew heavily upon Macy, *Dharma and Development,* and George D. Bond, *Buddhism at Work* (Bloomfield, CT: Kumarian Press, 2004).

P. 113.   Glassman's work with the Greyston Mandala: See Glassman and Fields, *Instructions to the Cook.*

Chapter 6: Ecology

P. 122.   Buddhism and ecology: On Buddhism and ecology, as well as for individual stories of environmental activists, I drew upon Kaza and Kraft, *Dharma Rain.*

P. 125.   John Seed: Biographical information is from *Inquiring Mind* 8, no. 2 (Spring 1992): 1, 6–7.

P. 126.   Gary Snyder: See his *The Practice of the Wild,* esp. "The Etiquette of Freedom."

P. 128.   Joanna Macy: I drew upon Macy, *World as Lover, World as Self.*

P. 130.   Ecology monks: I have largely drawn upon the work of Susan Darlington. See, for example, "The Ordination of a Tree: The Buddhist Ecology Movement in Thailand," *Ethnology* 37, no. 1 (Winter 1998): 1–15; available at http://ccbs.ntu.edu.tw/FULLTEXT/JR-ADM/susan.htm.

Chapter 7: Human Rights and Criminal Justice

P. 153.   Angulimala: For the story, see the *Aṅgulimāla Sutta* in Bhikkhu Ñāṇamoli and Bhikkhu Bodhi, *The Middle Length Discourses of the Buddha,* pp. 710–717.

P. 154.   Stultz: See Virginia Cohn Parkum and J. Anthony Stultz, "Symbol and Narration in Buddhist Prison Ministry," in *Action Dharma: New Studies in Engaged Buddhism,* ed. Christopher Queen et al. (New York: RoutledgeCurzon, 2003), pp. 240–241.

P. 156.   Melody Ermachild Chavis: For her reflections on her work, see her "Seeking Evil, Finding Only Good," in Moon, *Not Turning Away,* pp. 81–89, and "The 10,000 Causes of Crime," *Turning Wheel* (Summer 2001): 17–21.

P. 157.   The Dalai Lama on the lack of love in criminals' lives: See his *Ethics for the New Millennium,* pp. 64–65.

Chapter 8: Challenging Tradition

P. 160.   Ambedkar's understanding of the Buddha's teachings: See Christopher S. Queen, "Dr. Ambedkar and the Hermeneutics of Buddhist Liberation," in Queen and King, *Engaged Buddhism.*

P. 165.   Susan Moon: For her comments see *Turning Wheel* (Summer 2001): 2.

P. 165.   Melody Ermachild Chavis: See her "The 10,000 Causes of Crime."

P. 167.   Decline of the bhikkhuni order: See Nancy Auer Falk, "The Case of the Vanishing Nuns: The Fruits of Ambivalence in Ancient Indian Buddhism," in *Unspoken Worlds: Women's Religious Lives in Non-Western Cultures,* ed. Nancy A. Falk and Rita M. Gross (San Francisco: Harper and Row, 1980), pp. 207–224.

For Further Reading

A Selected List

ANTHOLOGIES

The following anthologies are especially useful in that every chapter in each of them is an account of a particular Engaged Buddhist leader or group and is written by someone who has extensively studied the subject. Therefore, one is able to access an informed, in-depth study of many different leaders and groups in each volume, gaining both breadth and depth.

Chappell, David W., ed. *Buddhist Peacework: Creating Cultures of Peace.* Somerville, MA: Wisdom Publications, 1999.

Kaza, Stephanie, and Kenneth Kraft, eds. *Dharma Rain: Sources of Buddhist Environmentalism.* Boston and London: Shambhala Publications, 2000.

Moon, Susan. *Not Turning Away: The Practice of Engaged Buddhism.* Boston and London: Shambhala Publications, 2004.

Queen, Christopher S., ed. *Engaged Buddhism in the West.* Boston: Wisdom Publications, 2000.

Queen, Christopher S., and Sallie B. King, eds. *Engaged Buddhism: Buddhist Liberation Movements in Asia.* Albany: State University of New York Press, 1996.

ASIAN LEADERS' WORKS

Dalai Lama, His Holiness the. *Ethics for the New Millennium.* New York: Riverhead Books, 1999.

Ghosananda, Maha. *Step by Step: Meditations on Wisdom and Compassion.* Berkeley, CA: Parallax Press, 1992.

Nhat Hanh, Thich. *Being Peace.* Berkeley, CA: Parallax Press, 1987.

———. *Love in Action: Writings on Nonviolent Social Change.* Berkeley, CA: Parallax Press, 1993.

Sulak Sivaraksa. *Seeds of Peace: A Buddhist Vision for Renewing Society.*
  Berkeley, CA: Parallax Press, 1992.

Suu Kyi, Aung San. *Freedom from Fear and Other Writings.* London:
  Penguin Books, 1991.

Swearer, Donald K., ed. *Me and Mine: Selected Essays of Bhikkhu
  Buddhadasa.* Albany: State University of New York Press, 1989.

WESTERN LEADERS' WORKS

Glassman, Bernie. *Bearing Witness: A Zen Master's Lessons in Making
  Peace.* New York: Bell Tower, 1998.

Macy, Joanna. *World as Lover, World as Self.* Berkeley, CA: Parallax
  Press, 1991.

Snyder, Gary. *The Practice of the Wild.* San Francisco: North Point
  Press, 1990.

STUDIES

Chappell, David W. *Socially Engaged Spirituality: Essays in Honor of
  Sulak Sivaraksa on His 70th Birthday.* Bangkok: Sathirakoses-
  Nagapradipa Foundation, 2003.

Jones, Ken. *The New Social Face of Buddhism: A Call to Action.* Boston:
  Wisdom Publications, 2003.

King, Sallie B. *Being Benevolence: The Social Ethics of Engaged Buddhism.*
  Honolulu: University of Hawai'i Press, 2005.

Kraft, Kenneth, ed. *Inner Peace, World Peace: Essays on Buddhism and
  Nonviolence.* Albany: State University of New York Press, 1992.

Loy, David. *The Great Awakening: A Buddhist Social Theory.* Somerville,
  MA: Wisdom Publications, 2003.

Macy, Joanna. *Dharma and Development: Religion as Resource in the
  Sarvodaya Self-Help Movement.* West Hartford, CT: Kumarian Press,
  1983.

Sulak Sivaraksa, ed. *Socially Engaged Buddhism for the New Millennium:
  Essays in Honor of the Ven. Phra Dhammapitaka (Bhikkhu P. A.
  Payutto) on His 60th Birthday Anniversary.* Bangkok: Sathirakoses-
  Nagapradipa Foundation and Foundation for Children, 1999.

JOURNALS

Journal of Buddhist Ethics (online journal): www.buddhistethics.org
Seeds of Peace (from Sulak Sivaraksa and International Network of
    Engaged Buddhists)
Turning Wheel: The Journal of Socially Engaged Buddhism (from
    Buddhist Peace Fellowship)
Yasodhara: Newsletter on International Buddhist Women's Activities
    (from Venerable Dhammananda)

WEB SITES

Buddhist Peace Fellowship: www.bpf.org
Dalai Lama, His Holiness the: www.tibet.com
Dhammananda, Venerable: www.thaibhikkhunis.org
Glassman, Bernie: www.zenpeacemakers.org
Macy, Joanna: www.joannamacy.net
Nhat Hanh, Thich: www.plumvillage.org
Ouyporn Khuankaew: www.womenforpeaceandjustice.org
Sarvodaya Shramadana: www.sarvodaya.org *and*
    www.sarvodayaUSA.org
Sulak Sivaraksa: www.sulak-sivaraksa.org/en
Think Sangha: www.bpf.org/think.html
Tzu Chi: www.tzuchi.org/global

Index

Ambedkar, Dr. B. R., 11, 145–146, 160–161
Amidon, Elias, 104
anātman. See no-self
Angulimala, 153–154
animals: protection of, 26, 74, 98, 99, 119–121, 135–136, 139; understanding of, 21, 71, 120, 123
Ariyaratne, Dr. A. T., 5, 9–10; development work of, 99, 105–114; peace-making work of, 89–90. *See also* Sarvodaya Shramadana
Auschwitz, 62–63
Avalokitesvara, 24, 68. *See also* Kuan Yin
awakening, 154; in Sarvodaya, 106, 111–112. *See also* Buddhahood; enlightenment; liberation, concept of

being with others, 51–53
bhikkhu. *See* monk
bhikkhuni issue, 167–173. *See also* gender
bodhicitta, 24
bodhisattva, 23–24, 61, 68, 78–79, 121, 155
Buddha, 8–9; and attitudes towards the world, 40–44, 148; on ecology, 118–121; on economics, 96–99; on gender, 166, 170–171; on karma, 159–165; key teachings of, 9, 13–27, 56–57, 84; on social class, 146
Buddhadasa Bhikkhu, 44–45, 59, 84
Buddhahood, 21–22, 107, 139. *See also* awakening; enlightenment; liberation, concept of
Buddhism, Engaged: Buddhist nature of, 12, 176–178; definition of, 1–2; justification of, 8–12; as response to crisis, 2–3; Western influence on, 11–12

Buddhist Peace Fellowship, 32
Buddhists, gay, 35
Burma, 6, 32; attitudes towards karma, 161–162, 165; human rights in, 138, 142–143; monks demonstrating in, 143–145. *See also* Suu Kyi, Aung San

Cakkavatti Sīhanāda Sutta, 99
Cambodia, 91–95. *See also* Maha Ghosananda
caste, 11, 21, 145–147, 160–161. *See also* dalits
causality, 13–14, 19, 20, 29, 33, 69–70, 99, 177–178; in Burma, 144; in criminal justice, 157–158; and ecology, 118; in Sarvodaya Shramadana, 37–38, 84–86, 88–89; in Thich Nhat Hanh, 82. *See also* interdependence; karma; origination, dependent
chanda, 20–21, 65–66
Chavis, Melody Ermachild, 156–158, 165–166
Cheng Yen, Venerable, 6, 24, 55–56. *See also* Tzu Chi
compassion, 8–9, 22–27, 32, 36–37, 39, 49–51; Cheng Yen on, 24, 55–56, 60–61; Dalai Lama on, 68, 71–72. *See also* love; loving-kindness
consumerism, 102–105, 116–117, 138
conversion, 146–148
Council of All Beings, 129–130
craving, 14–15, 20, 43, 45; and disabilities, 163–164; and economics, 97, 100, 103, 110
Cutts, Jiko Linda, 32–33

Dalai Lama, the, 4, 10, 31, 140; and compassion, 68, 71–72; and economics, 101; and love, 50, 157–158; and Tibet, 67–76; and universalism, 58–59, 64–66

dalits, 145–148, 160–161. *See also* Ambedkar, Dr. B. R.
dāna. See giving
Dao, 122, 126
dasarājadhamma, 41–42
deforestation, 74, 94, 103, 130–135
delusion, 13–14, 16, 22, 43. *See also* ignorance
Dhammananda, Venerable, 36, 170–173
Dhammapada, the, 68–69, 76, 79
Dhammayietra, 5, 91–95
disability, 163–164
Dogen, 122, 133
duḥkha, 9, 14–18, 20, 22, 41, 43, 58; in Ambedkar, 161; in Buddhadasa, 44–45, 84; and consumerism, 103, 106
dukkha. See *duḥkha*

ecology, 102–103, 109; deep, 122–130; of Thailand, 130–133; of Tibet, 73–74. *See also* forest; nature
empowerment, 164, 165; in Glassman, 114; in Macy, 128–129; in Sarvodaya, 107–108, 112
emptiness, 45–46, 55, 121
enlightenment, 40, 56, 139, 143, 146, 174; of Buddha, 8–10; concept of, 15–17, 21, 22; in Mahayana, 120–122. *See also* awakening; Buddhahood; liberation, concept of
ethics, developmental, 31
exclusivism, religious, 64

faith, 17
Fire Sermon, 40, 42
Five-Point Peace Plan, 73–74
forest, 119, 125–126. *See also* deforestation; trees, ordination of
Foundations of Mindfulness Sutta, 41
Four Noble Truths, 14–18, 37, 84–85, 103, 106
friendliness, inter-religious, 56–66
Friends of the Western Buddhist Order, 147–148
fundamentalism, 65

Gandhi, Mahatma, 2, 11, 68, 122
gender, 21, 146, 162–163, 166–175; in Sarvodaya, 107, 110

giving, 8, 23–24, 26–27, 46–47, 79, 98, 177; in Sarvodaya, 89, 108; in Tzu Chi, 55–56
Glassman, Roshi Bernie, 7; and bearing witness retreats, 62–63; and economics, 113–117; and street retreats, 51–55
Goenka, S. N., 152–154
Gollin, Jim, 134–135
Greyston Mandala, 7, 113–117

homelessness, 52–55, 113–115. *See also* poverty

ignorance, 15–17, 20, 36, 72, 77, 119. *See also* delusion
interdependence, 13–14, 19, 22, 25, 29, 45, 56; and ecology, 118–119, 121, 123; and economics, 97, 109, 111, 114. *See also* causality; karma
Israel, 35–36, 70

justice: criminal, 149–158, 177; economic, 101–102; political, 11, 35–38, 84, 93, 140, 178; retributive, 35, 149

Kabilsingh, Chatsumarn. *See* Dhammananda, Venerable
karma, 8, 13–14, 21, 23–25, 30, 131; attitudes towards in Burma, 144, 161–162, 165; attitudes towards in Cambodia, 93; attitudes towards in Tibet, 36; challenges to, 159–166; and criminal justice, 149, 157–158; and dalits, 160–161; and disabilities, 163–164; and gender, 162–163, 167, 173; and nonviolence, 68–71, 79, 85–86, 93. *See also* causality
karuṇā. See compassion
Kaza, Stephanie, 102
Kuan Yin, 61. *See also* Avalokitesvara

liberation, concept of, 14, 16, 40–45. *See also* awakening; Buddhahood; enlightenment
Livelihood, Right, 97–98; in Glassman, 115–117
Loori, John Daido, 133–134, 150–151
love, 51; in Bernie Glassman, 53; in the Dalai Lama, 50, 71, 158; in Maha

Ghosananda, 50; of nature, 119, 128, 133; in Thich Nhat Hanh, 49–50, 61, 79, 81; in Tzu Chi, 55, 60–61. *See also* compassion; loving-kindness

loving-kindness, 3, 22–23, 26–27, 41–42, 49–51; in Dhammayietra, 92–93; in Sarvodaya, 86–87, 111. *See also* compassion; love

Loy, David, 102–103

Macy, Joanna, 7, 128–130

Maha Ghosananda, 5, 50, 79; and peacemaking, 71, 91–95

Masters, Jarvis Jay, 156

Maull, Fleet, 156

meditation, 10, 40–42, 48–51, 63, 104, 125; in Cambodia, 93; graveyard, 41, 49; in prison, 149–153; in Sarvodaya peacemaking, 86–88, 111; in Thailand, 103–104; in Thich Nhat Hanh, 83, 124. *See also* mindfulness

mettā. See loving-kindness

Mettā Sutta, 41, 93

Middle Path, 97–100, 105–106

Miller, Brad, 135

mindfulness, 33, 41, 104, 128, 174; in Glassman, 54–55, 114, 116; in Thich Nhat Hanh, 48–49, 77, 82–83, 104, 124, 155. *See also* meditation

monk: development, 5, 103–104, 113; ecology, 5–6, 130–133; forest/village dwelling, 10, 40–41, 119

Moon, Susan, 165

Myanmar. *See* Burma

Naess, Arne, 122–123

National Buddhist Prison Sangha, 150–151

nationalism, Buddhist, 3

National Prison Hospice Association, 156

nature, 119–121; in Daoism, 122; in Gary Snyder, 126–128; as loved, 119, 128, 133; in Zen Mountain Monastery, 133–134. *See also* animals; ecology; forest

Nature, Buddha, 21–22, 65–66, 153–154

nature, human, 18–22, 71, 106, 127, 157

Nhat Chi Mai, 61

Nhat Hanh, Thich, 4–5, 8, 11, 168; and

Buddhist precepts, 26–27, 104–105; and criminal justice work, 155; and ecology, 118–119, 124–125; and love, 49–50, 61; and nonjudgmentalism, 27–30; and peacemaking, 32, 76–83, 176; and spiritual practices, 48–49; and universalism, 59–60

nirvana, 15–17, 43, 56–57, 121

Nobel Peace Prize, 4, 6

nonadversariality, 30–32, 37, 138–139, 177

nondualism, 121–123, 126–127

nonenmity, 31–32; in Dalai Lama, 50, 72–73; in Thich Nhat Hanh, 77, 81–82

nonjudgmentalism, 27–38, 52, 82, 177

nonviolence, 24–27, 139, 178; in Burma, 142–145; in Cambodia, 91–95; in Sri Lanka, 83–90; in Tibet, 68–76, 141; in Vietnam, 76–83. *See also* peace

no-self, 18–22, 68–69, 176; and ecology, 119–120, 123–126; and human rights, 138; and nonadversariality, 31; and nonjudgmentalism, 34, 37; and nonviolence, 24–25, 29, 71–72; and precepts, 30–31. *See also* self

not-knowing, 52–53

nuclear guardianship, 128

origination, dependent, 13–14, 15, 118–119, 123. *See also* causality; karma

Ouyporn Khuankaew, 173–174

Palmers, Vanya, 135–136

Parable of the Raft, 56–57, 60

peace, 12; being, 81, 176; inner, 40, 48, 87, 93, 133. *See also* nonviolence; peacemaking

Peace Brigade, 111

Peace Council, 35–37

peacemaking: and inter-religious friendliness, 61–63; in Sarvodaya, 37–38, 50. *See also* nonviolence

People's Peace Plan, 37–38, 84–88

poverty, 11, 96, 98–102, 160–161; in Glassman, 113–116; in Sarvodaya, 84–85, 110–111; in TBMSG, 147–148. *See also* wealth

precepts, 24–27, 30–31, 35, 79; and consumerism, 103–104; in Dham-

mayietra, 95; and ecology, 120–121; and human rights, 138–139, 141–142; in prison work, 152, 154; in Thich Nhat Hanh, 60, 104–105, 155
Prison Dharma Network, 156
prisons, 149–158; Goenka's work in, 152–153; Zen Mountain Monastery work in, 150–151
punishment, capital, 150, 156–158

Quang Duc, Thich, 78–79

reconciliation, 31–32, 61, 68, 71, 85, 88, 91, 94, 178
relations, inter-religious, 56–66
retreats, bearing witness, 62–63; street, 52–55
rights, human, 137–148; in Burma, 138, 142–143; in Cambodia, 141–142; case against, 137–138; in dalit Buddhist movement, 145–147; defense of, 138–140; of self-development toward Buddhahood, 139; in Tibet, 73, 140–141

sacred-profane dualism, 121–123, 127
samsara, 8, 16, 40–45, 49, 97, 120–122
Sarvodaya Shramadana, 5, 37–38, 50, 57, 128; development program of, 105–113; peacemaking effort of, 84–90
Seed, John, 125–126, 129
self, 18–22, 66; and other, 31, 45–47, 51–56, 177; and spiritual practice, 47–48; as world, 128–130. See also no-self
self-interest, 30–31, 71
self-immolation, 61, 78–79
selflessness, 58–59, 64. See also no-self; self
Sharp, Gene, 145
Sigālovāda Sutta, 41
Skill in Means Sutra, 79
Snyder, Gary, 126–127

Sopa, Geshe, 36–37
Sri Lanka, 3, 10, 25, 83–90, 105–113. See also Sarvodaya Shramadana
Struggle Movement, Vietnamese, 76–81
Stultz, Anthony, 154
Sulak Sivaraksa, 59, 102–103, 110
Suu Kyi, Aung San, 6, 11, 32, 142; and human rights, 139, 142–143; and karma, 161–162, 165
Suzuki, Shunryu, 52

Taiwan, 6. See also Cheng Yen, Venerable
TBMSG, 147–148
Thailand, 25, 103; bhikkhuni order in, 170–173; development monks in, 5, 103–104, 113; ecology monks in, 5–6, 130–133; sex trade in, 162, 169
"thusness," 120
Tibet, 4, 36–37, 67–76, 138, 140–141, 145. See also Dalai Lama, the
trees, ordination of, 131–132. See also forest; nature
Tzu Chi, 6, 24, 27, 55–56, 60–61

Unified Buddhist Church of Vietnam, 76
universalism, Buddhist, 56–66

value, instrumental and intrinsic, 119–121
Vietnam, 4–5, 31–32, 49, 61, 76–83. See also Nhat Hanh, Thich

war. See peacemaking
wealth, 98–101, 106, 138. See also poverty
work camp, 108, 110–112

Zen Mountain Monastery, 133–134, 150–151
Zen Peacemaker Order, 7, 52–53. See also Glassman, Roshi Bernie

About the Author

Sallie B. King is professor of philosophy and religion at James Madison University in Harrisonburg, Virginia. Among her many publications on Buddhism, Engaged Buddhism, Buddhist-Christian dialogue, and the cross-cultural philosophy of religion are *Engaged Buddhism: Buddhist Liberation Movements in Asia* (co-edited with Christopher Queen) and *Being Benevolence: The Social Ethics of Engaged Buddhism* (University of Hawaiʻi Press, 2005).

Production Notes for King / SOCIALLY ENGAGED BUDDHISM

Interior design by Rich Hendel; cover design by Santos Barbasa, Jr.

Composition by Josie Herr

Printing and binding by Versa

Printed on 60# Accent Opaque, 435 ppi